ADVANC

"Sales targets are challenging and ever increasing, so you have to get better—the strategies outlined in this book will help you succeed. Greg brings his extensive experience to create a thoughtful and fresh perspective on sales execution and strategy. A very worthwhile read."

—ROBERT COURTEAU, BOARD MEMBER AND EXECUTIVE ADVISOR, FORMER PRESIDENT NORTH AMERICA AND GLOBAL CHIEF OPERATING OFFICER, SAP

"Greg worked with our sales team to implement many of the P3 Selling concepts. Its structured approach fosters results. I would recommend it to any sales leader looking to take their team to the next level."

—HEATHER JOHNSON, CHIEF EXECUTIVE OFFICER, INGENIUM

"A concise and logical approach to excel in today's competitive and complex B2B selling environment. P3 Selling details the key elements necessary to optimize sales productivity and predictability for sales professionals and their leaders that would otherwise take years of training and experience to learn."

—DAVE BOWMAN, FOUNDER, DRB SALES MASTERY, FORMER VICE PRESIDENT, TELUS COMMUNICATIONS

"Greg worked with our global sales team on being more strategic. P3 Selling offers more solid advice on how to positively differentiate both yourself and your company from the competition so that you win more deals."

—JERRY OLECHIW, VICE PRESIDENT GLOBAL SALES AND MARKETING, DOBLE ENGINEERING

P3 SELLING

P3 Selling^{SM}

THE ESSENTIALS OF B2B SALES SUCCESS

Greg Nutter

LIONCREST
PUBLISHING

P3 SELLING
The Essentials of B2B Sales Success

FIRST EDITION

ISBN   978-1-5445-2998-1 *Hardcover*
        978-1-5445-2997-4 *Paperback*
        978-1-5445-2999-8 *Ebook*

CONTENTS

INTRODUCTION 11

1. DEFINE "SELLING" 17

2. P1: PROBLEMS 37

3. P2: PEOPLE 59

4. P3: PROCESSES 81

5. P3 SELLING PLAYBOOK 109

6. THE JOURNEY BEYOND 161

   P3 SELLING RESOURCES............................ 171

   NOTES 173

INTRODUCTION

You Never Want to be "THAT Guy"!

Early in my sales career, I came across a situation I never wanted to be in. It scared the crap out of me. I was working for a division of Xerox that sold computer hardware and software to corporate data centers. While Xerox primarily hired their office equipment sellers right out of college, they preferred to hire more-tenured reps for this division so they would command more customer credibility. One hire was a very well-dressed, articulate, mid-thirties to early-forties gentlemen who looked every bit the part of a successful seller. We all thought he was going to do well, as he exuded enthusiasm and a lot of self-confidence. But as he began to call on his assigned accounts, he became very frustrated and angry. His problem? He couldn't get his customers to engage with him on any sales opportunities. As time went on, he became more and more critical of every customer he spoke to, blaming them for not wanting to work with him. And his feelings of anger began to shift to fear. He probably had success earlier in his career, maybe at a fast-growing company with a hot, new product or perhaps just a streak of good luck, but now, he seemed to forget how to make things happen. So here he was, a man without a clue on how to turn things around, and all he could see in front of him was failure. After only a few months on the job, he was fired. I wondered how long he would be on the streets after such a short stint and how long he would last at his next sales job. Whatever happened, my gut told me that it probably wasn't good.

Looking at him scared me to death so much that I decided I never wanted to be "that guy." So I spent a lot of time learning as much as I could about selling. I read all the popular books, took all the courses, and even became a sales trainer so I could see how well these best-practice techniques worked in action. But after studying all the different selling methodologies and programs, it struck me that there didn't seem to be a single source that captured all the key success factors in one cohesive package. Lots of good ideas on processes, tips, and techniques, but they were largely unconnected and never the full picture. More than just "some assembly required."

Fortunately, over time, I was able to piece these essential elements together myself and avoided my colleague's frightening situation. However, throughout my career as a sales leader and consultant, I continued to come across many sellers who had also lost their way, didn't know where to turn, and were living day to day with the stress and fear of not making their numbers and losing their jobs. It was for these people that I decided to write this book—a single resource with all the critical success elements connected and in one place—in order to help keep them from becoming "that guy"!

A SELLER'S CHALLENGE

Everyone who pursues a career in sales wants both the prestige and financial rewards of success. But figuring out how to achieve success often isn't an easy journey. Sure, there are many books, blog posts, and websites out there, along with co-workers and friends who offer free advice. But many of these tips and techniques seem gimmicky, manipulative, or even outright shady. Worst of all, a lot of them don't work. There are also professional sales-training companies that offer time-consuming and often expensive training workshops. But in my experience, most people who attend them struggle to use the concepts afterward and don't get any lasting benefit. So while we're drowning in complex jargon, proprietary models, and insider tips on how to succeed, for many, this body of knowledge simply isn't working.

As a result, many professional sellers experience inconsistent results, the constant fear of missing their sales targets, and a nagging lack of confidence in responding to high-risk/high-payoff selling situations. If this sounds a little like you, let me congratulate you on picking up the right book.

WHAT'S P3 SELLING?

P3 Selling is an easy-to-follow, prescriptive framework that describes what you need to do and why you need to do it to achieve consistent B2B sales success. By learning and applying these concepts regularly, you will experience:

- Greater self-confidence in your knowledge and ability to navigate today's complex B2B selling environment;

- More success in winning deals, receiving referrals, making money, and getting promoted to senior sales or sales-management positions; and

- A more profound sense of personal satisfaction resulting from having more control over achieving your goals versus hoping for a lucky break.

In reading this book, you'll develop a deep understanding of the three most critical B2B selling elements. Elements that you must consistently focus on to be successful. While most of the book is about selling strategy, I'll also share a few non-manipulative, but highly useful, techniques to benefit your sales interactions. What you'll find missing is the complexity and unnecessary jargon typically found in other sales-training programs.

Also, at the end of each chapter, I'll suggest some activities you can use to apply these concepts to your own unique selling situation.

WHY P3 SELLING

In my thirty-plus years as a salesperson, sales trainer, sales leader, consultant, and coach, I've worked with over a thousand sales professionals who have struggled to find a consistent, predictable, and comprehensive formula to enable their success. In working with them, I often came across the same set of gaps in understanding about how top sellers succeed. Yet, by focusing them on just three foundational concepts, many saw an immediate improvement in their performance. This book reveals these critical concepts in a simple, straightforward manner to facilitate that elusive formula for success.

For those new to sales, *P3 Selling* offers a practical and easy-to-follow selling approach you can use right away to start achieving results. For tenured sales professionals, it provides a refresher on the most critical selling success factors that made you successful earlier in your careers. And for sales leaders, *P3 Selling* offers a comprehensive sales methodology you can use to manage your sales teams more effectively through a consistent set of strategies and processes.

Whatever your experience level, *P3 Selling* will be a valuable resource you can refer to on an ongoing basis, particularly when faced with a challenging sales situation.

If this sounds like what you've been looking for, then let's begin our journey by asking what appears to be a simple question—but isn't. Read on!

CHAPTER 1

DEFINE "SELLING"

"Never confuse activity with accomplishment."
—JOHN WOODEN

What exactly IS "Selling"? Ask anyone to define selling, and for sure, you won't have a problem getting a quick answer. The challenge is that many responses aren't very constructive. I recently asked a seller this question, and their reply was immediate. "It's getting someone to buy my stuff." *Nailed it!*

Sarcasm aside, the disconnect is not in the "what do we want" but in the "what should we do." And it is this "doing" part that's critical to understand if you want to get good at it. One definition defines selling as "to influence someone on the merits of something." But what you do to influence someone depends on the sales situation. So before we delve deeper into the "doing," let's begin with some differentiation.

SELLING IS SIMPLE UNTIL IT'S NOT

There are two different kinds of sales situations: Simple and

Complex. Some refer to these as "transactional sales" (Simple) and "solution sales" (Complex). Simple Sales involve the selling most of us are familiar with when purchasing as a consumer. As such, we refer to this kind of selling as Business to Consumer, or B2C. A Simple Sale involves either one of the following situations:

- The connection between product features and buyer benefits is pretty obvious, so they don't need much explaining. For example:
  - Product feature = lower cost than competitive products
  - Buyer's benefit = save money (pretty obvious)

OR

- The buying decision is made by a small number of people (often just one) with very few steps involved.

We're involved in Simple Sale decisions almost every day of our lives, like when we go to a store to buy electronics, appliances, clothes, food, and restaurant meals.

A Complex Sale is the opposite of a Simple Sale, where either one of the following situations is true:

- The connection between product features and buyer benefits is not obvious, even after much explaining (Product Complexity). For example:
  - Product feature = pay an ongoing monthly subscription versus a sizeable onetime payment
  - Buyer's benefit = easier to manage monthly costs versus one big payment. But the monthly expenses add up to a

Simple ~ past *Complex ~ NOW*

more significant amount over time, while with the one-time expenditure, you're done (hmmmm—less obvious)

OR

- The buying decision is made by more people (let's say three or more), and many steps are involved (Buying Decision Complexity).

When you are selling a product or service to a company, Business to Business, or B2B, selling, you are almost always operating in a Complex Sale situation. This is detailed in the graphic below:

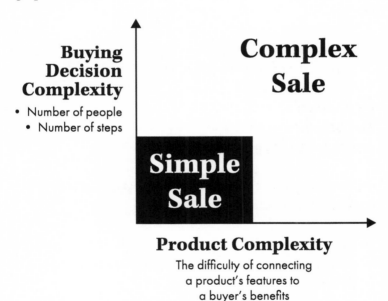

Buying Decision Complexity
- Number of people
- Number of steps

Complex Sale

Simple Sale

Product Complexity
The difficulty of connecting a product's features to a buyer's benefits

So why does this matter? Because the selling process and success factors are different for each.

For example, in a Simple Sale, the selling process is as follows:

1. Give information

workin ✗ 2. Ask for the order or the logical next step

If you don't get the order, you ask what additional information they need, then repeat the two steps above until you either get a NO or the order. Even if you get another NO, you can still go back and ask if they need more information before making a final decision. We see this kind of sales process play out every day:

- "We have a sale on fries today. Would you like me to include some with your order?"

- "We won't be able to keep this item in stock for very long. Would you like to place an order for it today?"

- "I'm guessing you don't want the risk of being without this policy. Should I get going on the paperwork for you?"

I call this way of selling "Clerking," as it's what most sellers do in a retail, or B2C, sales environment. And to be clear, Clerking can work as a viable selling process in certain situations, such as when:

- Your product or service is very simple

- Your product or service is obviously differentiated—e.g., a very low price

- You have a lot of sales opportunities, many more than you can handle

- There aren't, or the prospect isn't aware of, any real alternative options

- The buyer already knows what they want and is already sold

But if you are in B2B sales, you know this isn't your reality. Yet, in my experience, many B2B sellers act as if they are dealing with a Simple Sale. They give information and then ask for the order. And in fact, my guess is that:

CLERKING WINS AS MANY AS 20 PERCENT OR MORE OF B2B SALES. THE PROBLEM IS THAT THERE IS A HIGH PROBABILITY OF LOSING THE OTHER 80 PERCENT BY SELLING THIS WAY.

Some time ago, I went on a customer call with a sales rep that was a whiz at the Clerking method. He would meet with a potential prospect and, after a bit of small talk, whip out his binder that contained a brochure for each of his products. Then, he would slowly start flipping the pages while telling the customer, "Stop me if you see something you like." Hard to believe, I know. Predictably, he didn't last long.

Let me share a different example where this kind of selling "appears" to work. I spent some time coaching a sales director whose company offered a pretty complex service. He had done well as a sales rep before being promoted, even though his approach was mainly Clerking—giving information and then asking for the order. The reason why it worked for him was that he was an expert in his field. He would provide his prospects with all kinds of guidance on pitfalls to avoid and how to do their jobs better. This expertise gave him a higher degree of credibility than his competitors' reps. The approach often worked because his company's services, which included him, were highly and obviously differentiated. But not all customers want the same things. Those who valued this expertise would prefer to buy from him. But others, who appreciated lower prices, national support, or other capabilities, wouldn't care as much. Not only that, the day that one of his competitors hires a sales rep who's equally credible, that differentiation evaporates. That's why you can't consistently win with this kind of selling strategy.

Here's another observation: If you come across a seller's resume that shows a new employer every six months to a year, even when it highlights over-plan achievement in many of them, there's a good chance they were just Clerking. When the deals that others had mostly sold before the rep arrived get closed, it becomes tough to keep the good times rolling. So they either panic and leave or an astute sales manager figures out they're not up to the job and sends them packing.

Because we're so often exposed to Clerking as a consumer, we naturally—but mistakenly—assume it's the way to sell as a B2B sales professional. Instead, to win more predictably and consistently in a Complex Sale, you need to sell differently. So:

IF YOU ARE EVER IN DOUBT WHETHER YOU ARE DEALING WITH A SIMPLE SALE OR A COMPLEX SALE, ALWAYS START BY ASSUMING IT'S A COMPLEX SALE.

Bottom line: you use a Simple Sale selling process for a Complex Sale at your peril!

TELLING VERSUS SELLING

In order to sell or influence potential customers in a Complex Sale, you must first create awareness. An informal "law of awareness" was originally described by John C. Maxwell in his book *The 15 Invaluable Laws of Growth*. The idea is this: if you want to get someone to change, you need to increase their awareness of the current state. And selling, at its core, is all about influencing someone to change—change their thinking or change their situation.

REAL SELLING INVOLVES INCREASING A PROSPECT'S AWARENESS OF THEIR CURRENT STATE AND THUS THE NEED TO CHANGE, IN EFFECT, CREATING "LIGHTBULB MOMENTS."

You're probably wondering: in what areas are we trying to increase awareness? There are many: awareness of a particular problem or opportunity, awareness of the importance of addressing a problem, awareness of how one product is superior to another, or awareness around the best approach toward making a buying decision.

There are two ways you can try to create awareness: the easy and less effective way or the harder but considerably more powerful way. The easy way is to simply "tell." Here are some typical examples of what a seller might say:

- "It's important for you to consider that a panel of industry experts selected our product as the most innovative offering."

- "You'll be interested to learn more about our services because I'll bet your company is trying to save money this year."

- "When you make your buying decision, be sure to select a vendor with stability."

Telling is a salesperson's "go-to" behavior because it's easy to do, it's fast, and we all know how to do it. We see it every day, and because everyone does it, we think it works. It does—*in Simple Sales*. In a Complex Sale, giving information, or "telling," is surprisingly a lot less effective at creating awareness. In fact, buyers can perceive it as downright obnoxious. In my sales workshops, I tell people that:

AFTER ABOUT THE AGE OF TWO, NO ONE LIKES TO BE TOLD. IT'S SELLERS WHO ONLY KNOW HOW TO TELL THAT GIVE THE PROFESSION A BAD RAP.

So if you don't "tell," what exactly should you do? You ASK. Telling doesn't engage the mind as effectively as asking good questions does. We're often selling to busy executives with lots on their minds, so it's challenging to get them to focus on our ramblings (a.k.a. "telling"). I heard a great adage not too long ago that helps explain this—"multitasking is a myth." Research has shown that people are not good at doing or thinking about more than one thing at a time. Instead, what appears to be multitasking is actually switching back and forth between many tasks or thoughts very quickly. And when people do that, they tend not to be very good at processing either. This means that your exec will likely understand less than half of what you say unless you can somehow get them to focus their attention exclusively on you.

Let me give you a familiar example. You're at a conference or some other social setting, and someone you've never met comes up to you and tells you their name. More often than not, you forget it within just a few seconds because you weren't sufficiently engaged to focus on it. Perhaps you were busy thinking about what you would say next or how you might make a good impression, or you simply had other things on your mind. You were "multitasking," and you had no awareness that remembering their name was more important than the other things you were focusing on. The same thing happens on a sales call when a prospect listens to you talking about your stuff. Now instead, let's say the same person in our example comes up to you, tells you their name, and then immediately asks, "Can you guess where my last name comes from?" I would wager that your first response is to say, "Sorry, what was your name again?" Then when you hear it, you focus on their name and the question and stop thinking about anything else. As a result, you are much more likely to remember their name because the question created awareness of its importance.

SALES PLAY: ASK↔SUGGEST:RECAP (ASR)

As I mentioned earlier, along with providing you with the essential selling strategies you need to be successful, I also want to share a few non-manipulative techniques to help you implement these strategies during your sales interactions. I call these Sales Plays. The first Sales Play I want to introduce is called the Ask↔Suggest:Recap, or ASR, model.

A ton of research shows that asking is a far more powerful way to influence versus telling because it gets people to focus, think, and become more aware. So while we use an iterative, two-step process in Simple Sales, we use the following three-step process in Complex Sales:

1. Ask

2. Suggest

3. Recap

Graphically, it looks like this:

Ask   Suggest ⟶ Recap

- Ask & Explore
  - Problems & Opportunities
  - Importance

- Validate
- Suggest & Explain
- Ask for Agreement

- Summarize
- Confirm

Here's how the Ask ⟷ Suggest:Recap, or ASR, Sales Play works:

1. **Ask.** Start by Asking about something important to know for your sale. It can be how much they spend on a particular service or how many employees they have. Once you have some initial information, Explore further to understand what's working for them and what's not. The goal is to find associated problems or opportunities that your offerings can address. Each of these problems or opportunities, from a selling perspective, is a nugget of gold. Then, Ask about the importance and urgency of solving them, either personally or for others within their organization. Asking by itself creates awareness. But let's say they lack awareness in areas that differentiate what you sell from your competition. Proceed to the next step.

trial close

2. **Suggest.** Suggesting can create awareness in areas that the prospect hadn't considered. Start by Validating what they've told you. Something like, "I fully understand why you would want the cheapest offering, but could I share another perspective with you?" And then Suggest a different perspective and Ask if they would agree. Perhaps you'll Suggest that while price is really important, ongoing costs are important as well. Explain why this is a significant consideration, and then Ask if they would agree with your Suggestion. If they agree, great—if they don't, you could try again with a different explanation. But if they don't agree with any of the reasoning you Suggest, move on. After a few cycles of Asking and Suggesting, move to another topic, and start digging for more gold.

3. **Recap.** Once you've captured enough problem and opportunity nuggets, move to the Recap step. Summarize what you've heard, and Ask for the prospect to Confirm that they agree.

This ASR cycle creates awareness in several ways. First, just asking people about problems or opportunities makes them top of mind. Secondly, probing the importance of addressing them encourages people to assess whether they should take action. Suggesting takes this one step further by getting people to think of things they may not have considered. Now, this isn't some "Jedi mind-trick" because all you're doing is suggesting a different perspective in a very respectful way. Often, this creates a new awareness and thus a change in perspective.

> *"The art of advice is to make the recipient*
> *believe he thought of it himself."*
>
> —FRANK TYGER

But if they disagree, they will tell you so, which will be the end of it. Once you have exhausted a particular topic area, wrap things up through a brief recap and ask to confirm. This step is essential, as it pulls together all the gold nuggets into a single package. By themselves, each nugget might not be persuasive enough to motivate a prospect to take action. Altogether, they can represent a very compelling argument for change.

While going through the ASR cycle, it's vital to resist the urge to start telling or Clerking, as they can bring an end to your conversation faster than you might like. In my experience, telling is one of the fastest ways to get an objection.

Let me illustrate the difference between Clerking and selling by using a scenario that we're probably all familiar with—buying a car.

Clerking:

SALESPERSON: Welcome to our showroom—how can we help you?

PROSPECT: I'm thinking of buying a new car.

SALESPERSON: Sounds good—we've got some excellent deals going on right now. Are you planning on making your purchase today?

PROSPECT: Actually, I'm just looking, thanks. <Disengages and walks away>

Selling using the ASR Sales Play (Ask ↔ Suggest:Recap):

SALESPERSON: Welcome to our showroom—how can we help you?

PROSPECT: I'm thinking of buying a new car.

SALESPERSON: Sounds good—what kind of car are you driving now?

PROSPECT: I've got this old two-door that I picked up while in college, but I think it's time for a change.

SALESPERSON: What is it about your current car that's not meeting your needs?

PROSPECT: It's constantly breaking down, so I need something that won't cost me a fortune in repair bills.

SALESPERSON: So reliability is really important for you—what else?

PROSPECT: I don't want to spend too much, so whatever is reliable and cheap is what I'm after.

SALESPERSON: Will you be the only person in the car?

PROSPECT: Mostly, but I'm married and have two small children.

SALESPERSON: Ah, that's good to know. I understand the importance of keeping costs down, but cheap cars often don't have the best safety features. Many people with small families find these features really important. Would this be something you might want to factor into your decision?

PROSPECT: Hmmm—I hadn't thought of that. Yes, I think that's a pretty important consideration.

<More Asking, Exploring, Suggesting>

SALESPERSON: Great. So from what you've told me, reliability, low cost, and good safety features are the most important things we should be looking for—is that correct?

PROSPECT: Yes, I think you've summarized it well.

As you can see from the selling example, it is far from being manipulative. On the contrary, it actually increases your credibility in the eyes of the prospect because most prospect value sellers ask thought-provoking questions instead of just telling them what they think. And only the prospect's perspective matters, even when you think they should consider other options. Thus, this technique is at the center of a genuine consultative selling approach.

In the following few chapters, I'll point out other key areas where you'll use this Sales Play to create greater awareness. While it seems relatively straightforward, executing it well can be more challenging than it appears. Not to worry, though— you're in good hands.

ART, SCIENCE, OR JUST PLAIN LUCK

Many people see selling as an art or skill that you were either born with or without. Often, sales managers evaluate new hires based on whether they are outgoing, quick on their feet, a good conversationalist, and perhaps even fun—all the kinds of things we tend to think of as art. However, recent research around the science of selling has shown that consistently successful B2B sellers are highly process oriented. Less "winging it," more planned and deliberate.

What tips the scale is the answer to this question: are you involved in a Simple Sale or a Complex Sale? In a Simple Sale, you can do well by just being outgoing, friendly, and having some basic product knowledge. But in a Complex Sale, research shows that successful selling is much more of a science than art, although art can play a role. Complex Sales almost always play out over many selling interactions with a variety of different people. That's why using a sound, repeatable process is critical to achieving consistent success. Sometimes, you'll hear experienced sellers say that "people buy from people," which is to imply that relationship is the most important thing. There is undoubtedly some truth to this in a Simple Sale. But in today's Complex Sales, relationship is helpful but mostly not a deciding factor, as people can lose their jobs over making poor purchasing decisions. So if one salesperson's only attributes are that they are fun and outgoing, I'll go for lunch with them. But I'd rather buy from the person who asks the kinds of questions that will keep me out of trouble.

And of course, there's the luck component to selling, where certain aspects are pretty much a numbers game. But you can win more often by following a solid process.

*"The race is not always to the swift, nor the battle
to the strong, but that's the way to bet."*

—HUGH E. KEOUGH

P3 SELLING

The P3 Selling method provides a foundational strategy and system focused on the three most essential B2B sales-success elements. These elements are a prospect's Problems, People, and Processes as they relate to purchasing your products and services. In every selling interaction, your primary objective is to understand and influence each of these to increase the prospect's awareness of the unique value you can bring. In the next few chapters, we'll delve deeper into each element and provide more specifics on what to explore and how to influence each. While the primary influencing technique we'll be using is the ASR Sales Play (Ask↔Suggest:Recap), I'll also share a few others that can help with particularly challenging situations.

KEY TAKEAWAYS

To excel in any field, the starting point is to have clarity on the specific strategies and behaviors that lead to success. Selling is no different. However, B2B sales strategies are not always intuitive, leading sellers to do what comes naturally versus what will lead to the most successful outcomes. Here, I shared a few key perspectives and a Sales Play as starting points for that clarity.

There are two different kinds of sales you are likely to encounter: the Simple Sale and the Complex Sale. If you are selling to businesses, you will almost always be involved in a Complex Sale. That means either the connection between your offering's features and the buyer's benefits is not very obvious OR there are multiple people and steps involved in the buying decision. If you are ever in doubt, ALWAYS assume you are dealing with a Complex Sale.

Complex Sales require selling, not Clerking, where you just give people information and hope that they buy. Selling involves creating or enhancing a prospect's awareness, and the most powerful way to do this is by asking questions. And not just any questions but specifically those that create awareness in areas where you are trying to drive change.

Sellers who consistently follow a sound process win more often than those that don't. The P3 Selling method is just such a process that focuses sellers on the three essential elements of B2B selling success: Problems, People, and Processes.

The ASR Sales Play (Ask ↔ Suggest:Recap) is a practical, non-manipulative technique to create and enhance awareness in each buying-cycle stage. It also increases your credibility by asking prospects what they think instead of telling them what you think.

After you've completed the activities below, move on to our next chapter, where we'll dive deeper into P3 Selling's first key element: Problems.

MAKE IT YOUR OWN

The key to making P3 Selling work for you is to take the time to think through how you'll apply it in your unique situation. Start by asking yourself these questions:

- When you compare your offerings to the competition, how obvious is it to a prospect (not you) that your solutions are the better choice?

- When you're involved in a selling situation, who does most of the talking—you or the prospect?

- When you're on a sales call, how much time do you spend giving information versus asking about problems or opportunities?

- How structured are your selling efforts? For example, do you have a consistent process to guide you through each sales call and a prospect's buying process, or do you mostly react based on how things unfold?

After you've made a mental note of your answers, write a list of the top things you'd like to change about how you sell. You'll want to refer to this list for ideas on making these changes as you continue through the book.

CHAPTER 2

P1: PROBLEMS

*I don't know what I'm selling until I
know what you are buying.*

Of course, you know what you're selling. You're selling whatever your company has given you to sell, whether it's a product, a service, or a combination of the two. You've been through all the training on your company's history, product features, benefits, pricing, and competitive comparisons and are fully enabled to present it all. You are ready to roll!

A FOCUS ON PROBLEMS

But the fact is businesspeople don't buy products or services. They buy solutions that resolve problems or provide ways to capture new opportunities. Semantics, right? NO! This distinction is important because many sellers tend to drone on about their company's successes and their product's uniqueness, while customers mostly don't care. If you want a customer to listen and truly understand the value you can bring, you have to put your accolades into context with what they want to buy: a solution to a problem or a way to capture an opportunity. Collectively, we'll call both of these "Problems." So to truly be able to sell, you have to remember the following:

right to present ✗

YOU CANNOT SELL UNTIL YOU HAVE IDENTIFIED ONE OR MORE PROBLEMS THAT A PROSPECT WANTS TO ADDRESS—YOU CAN ONLY CLERK!

I'll go one step further. Without a well-defined need, you cannot have a logical discussion about products, services, costs, competition, or decision processes. It makes no sense—unless you are Clerking. So the first step in successful B2B selling is to uncover problems and opportunities your prospect wants to address. That's why the first pillar in P3 Selling is "Problems."

According to one definition, a problem is a situation preventing something from being achieved. It comes from a Greek word meaning "obstacle," or something that is in your way. Problems can be business or personal, although in reality, all business Problems are at their core "personal." People strive to address business Problems because, in doing so, they resolve personal Problems for themselves—Problems like hassle, stress, a poor review, or the risk of being fired. On the other hand, addressing business opportunities can create personal opportunities, like being promoted, enhancing your reputation, earning more money, going home early, or simply personal satisfaction. Earlier, we saw how selling, which is all about creating awareness, depends on asking questions. Many people believe they are good sellers because they ask a lot of questions. The issue is that, in many cases, they aren't asking enough of the right kinds of questions. They ask almost exclusively Fact questions. These

are questions about the cost of a particular service, the numb
of people employed, or the company's goals for the coming
year. Fact questions are important primarily as a launchpad into
asking good Problem questions. They give you context to point
you in the right direction. But Fact questions rarely create and
expand awareness of a buyer's need to change.

**MANY REPS STOP ASKING QUESTIONS AS SOON
AS THEY HAVE ENOUGH FACTS TO PUT TOGETHER
A QUOTE OR PROPOSAL—A RISKY MOVE.**

What's critical to the selling process is asking about Problems.
The more Problems you can find, the better chance you have of
influencing the need for change. Graphically, here is the field
where you'll be digging, along with some sample problem and
opportunity "gold nuggets" that you might ask about or suggest.

	Problems	Opportunities
Personal	• Stress • More work • Poor reviews • Long working hours • Demotion • Workplace conflict • Low job satisfaction	• Higher compensation • Promotion • Recognition • Greater career opportunities • Personal development • Reduced complexity • Job Security
Business	• Lower revenues/profits • Missed goals or targets • Regulatory fines • Cash constraints • Poor customer satisfaction • Poor employee satisfaction • Customer churn	• Faster growth • Greater profitability • Increased cash flow • Higher company valuation • Better employee retention • Increased renewal rates • Access new markets

Starting a sales call with a short company and product overview is okay, but you should resist going into detail. Afterward, quickly move to asking Fact questions to give you some context before heading into Problem questions. It's hard to jump right into asking Problem questions without some amount of situational knowledge. But be warned—prospects can find a lot of Fact questions tedious. Instead, do some research before your call so you can ask just enough to find clues on where to dig for Problems.

Once you've gathered enough Facts, start asking Problem questions that leverage what you learned. For example, if your prospect tells you their current service provider is raising rates by 15 percent (a Fact), you could probe further to see if they perceive this as a Problem. Something simple like "What do you think about that?" or "Does this concern you?" would work. The trap many sellers fall into is to _assume_ their prospect sees the increase as a problem. Instead of validating this, they start pitching how they could make the increase go away if the prospect bought from them. They begin Clerking to a Fact versus selling to a Problem.

assuming can fall into Clerking

UNTIL A PROSPECT EXPLICITLY TELLS YOU THAT A PARTICULAR SITUATION IS A PROBLEM, IT'S NOT.

The key is to uncover Problems you can solve and, ideally, solve better than your competitors. Here are a couple examples of what not to do. I was on a call with one salesperson where we were selling data-center printing systems—the kind of technology that allows companies to print large quantities of statements and invoices. The salesperson was very good at asking Problem questions, but he spent the first ten minutes probing Problems associated with a recent computer failure. Great dialogue was had, but the seller wasted scarce call time exploring a Problem we didn't have a solution to address.

Also, be careful exploring Problems where you don't have the best solution. A classic example is when a seller probes cost concerns when their offerings are rarely the cheapest. This strategy does a great job of raising awareness around the need to reduce costs, but it's a Problem that a competitor is more likely to solve.

Digging for Problems in the two Personal quadrants is often more successful in driving a buying decision. However, you'll need to establish some trust before exploring there. The safest way is to start asking about business-related Problems and then probe for personal linkages. For example, if your prospect expresses concern over their rising costs, you could simply ask, "How does this affect you personally?"

PROBLEM IMPORTANCE

The following situation may seem familiar. You had a great call with a prospect and gathered some good Facts and perhaps a few Problems. You then quickly put together a proposal and emailed it off the next day, only to have the buyer go silent on you. You then left a few voicemails and pinged them every other day asking for feedback. And you got nothing. Totally ghosted! That's because they found better things to spend their time on than responding to you. Even with a proposal focused on the exact Problems the prospect described, sellers can get no response. "What did I do wrong?" you might ask. Often, it's because the seller didn't create or expand awareness around the Importance of doing something. As a result, there was no motivation to respond. So pleas for them to return calls or emails only to give you an update become all about you, not them. Not very motivating.

Now, we know people do get busy at times and have to turn their attention to more urgent matters than looking over your quote. But if a seller probes further during those early calls, they have the means to motivate by reminding the prospect of the Importance of taking action. Different kinds of questions enable different things:

***

FACT QUESTIONS ENABLE YOU TO QUOTE.
PROBLEM QUESTIONS ENABLE YOU TO SELL.
QUESTIONS ABOUT IMPORTANCE
ENABLE YOU TO MOTIVATE.

***

Instead of the typical unmotivating voicemail or email—"Hi there, just checking in to see if you had any feedback on my proposal. Please call me back."—you can now leave a WIIFT (What's In It For Them) message versus a WIIFY (What's In It For You) message. Something like:

> Hi there, I wanted to reach out because you thought the <PROBLEMS> we discussed were pretty serious because of their <IMPACTS> and <URGENCY>.

I wondered if we could speak soon so we can help you get these resolved.

Note the difference in the WIIFT. You are far more likely to get a response when you remind people about *their* perceptions around the Importance of moving forward.

I like to emphasize to sellers that we all have many Problems—squeaky shoes, a leaky faucet, car wiper blades that smear, or maybe annoying bank fees. Or perhaps opportunities that we should take advantage of—like furthering our education or looking for a new job, both of which could improve our future prospects. But in reality, we choose to live with many of these problems or missed opportunities and never get around to addressing them. Companies are no different. We live in a busy world where we focus on some things and ignore the rest. So a critical thing to realize is the following:

⌈ JUST BECAUSE YOU UNCOVERED PROBLEMS DOES NOT *yes!* MEAN YOUR PROSPECT WILL DO ANYTHING ABOUT THEM. ⌋

If you've been in sales for any period of time, you know this to be true. At some point, you may have come across a prospect that had dismal support from their current supplier or could be growing their business twice as fast by investing in new technology. But for some reason, they just smile and never agree to change what they are doing. So to avoid these situations, after asking good Fact and Problem questions, you need to take one extra step. You have to understand and create greater awareness around the Importance of addressing each identified Problem. Think of it as "taking the temperature" of a Problem. The hotter it is, the greater the odds are that someone will take action to solve it.

A Problem's Importance is always about the **prospect's** perception, not yours. It's how they interpret the Impact—the cost of not resolving it or the benefit of resolving it—from either their business or personal standpoint. Although, as pointed out earlier, everything eventually gets perceived at the personal level. Depending on that perception, the problem or opportunity either gets prioritized for action or gets put aside. In addition to Impact, there's another dimension to a Problem's Importance—the Urgency to resolve it. Does it need to be done today, this month, this year, or just "at some point"? I like to describe this relationship as follows:

$$\left[\text{Importance} = \text{Impact} \times \text{Urgency} \right]$$

People regularly compare Problems to decide which to work on using these two factors. For example:

If I finish this report today, I will feel great about it and have a better chance of being promoted.

Versus:

If I come home late again, my spouse will be upset, but I'm sure they will understand. Probably best that I finish the report.

Most decisions on where to spend one's time aren't so obvious. And often, people get caught up in the urgent and easy stuff and don't spend enough time on the essential things. So your job as a salesperson is first to understand and then, if necessary, influence how the prospect perceives the Importance of resolving their Problems. And again, you don't do this by telling them what they should see as important. Instead, you do it by asking questions that create and increase their awareness.

You may wonder how questions about a Problem's Importance sound. My suggestion is that whenever you hear a prospect state a Problem, ask yourself, "So What?" While you will rarely say this directly, unless you have a very good relationship, you want to ask a less offensive "So What?" question every time your prospect tells you about a Problem. Also, try to get your prospect to quantify or attach a number to the "So What?" For example, do they perceive it to be a thousand-dollar problem, a hundred-thousand-dollar problem, or a million-dollar problem? That way, you'll have their "cost" estimate of not taking action. This cost can help you justify any price associated with addressing the Problem.

Here's an example of a situation you might encounter. Notice how the seller uses the ASR (Ask↔Suggest:Recap) Sales Play to raise awareness around both the Problem's Impact and Urgency:

> PROSPECT: Our costs for this service have been rising every year. <FACT>

> SALESPERSON: Does this concern you or others in your company?

> PROSPECT: For sure. We've been discussing this issue for some time. <PROBLEM>

> SALESPERSON: How important is it to get your costs either lower or at least stable?

PROSPECT: It's getting more critical. We estimate that we'll have to stop hiring new staff next year if we get another increase. <IMPACT>

SALESPERSON: How will that affect your business?

PROSPECT: It will undoubtedly constrain our ability to support new customers. <IMPACT>

SALESPERSON: In what ways?

PROSPECT: Today, it takes about thirty days to onboard a new customer. Without the new staff, we think it might double the time. <IMPACT>

SALESPERSON: I'll bet there's a financial hit to the company if that happens. Is that true?

PROSPECT: We hadn't thought about that, but you're probably right. If we can only onboard half of our planned new customers, we won't recognize the revenue from them. <IMPACT>

SALESPERSON: Wow, could that be big bucks?

PROSPECT: Absolutely—probably half a million dollars to the bottom line. <QUANTIFIED IMPACT>

SALESPERSON: Okay, so you're telling me that if you don't fix this problem before year-end, your profits will be down $500,000—is that correct? <RECAP>

PROSPECT: You're right—this is a big deal. We need to get this solved as soon as possible. <QUANTIFIED IMPACT × URGENCY = IMPORTANCE>

Here are a couple of comments on this scenario. First, note that the suggestions were subtle but essential in creating awareness that the Impact was significant. Also, the seller made no suggestions around Urgency; however, they should have if the prospect hadn't shared a looming deadline. Simply suggest one or more credible reasons why waiting isn't a good idea, and then ask if they agree. Finally, the prospect agreed with all the suggestions, but that doesn't always happen in real life. Let's make a small change to the scenario to see how the seller could respond.

> PROSPECT: Our costs for this service have been rising every year. <FACT>
>
> SALESPERSON: Does this concern you or others in your company?
>
> PROSPECT: For sure. We've been discussing this issue for some time. <PROBLEM>
>
> SALESPERSON: How important is it to get your costs either lower or at least stable?
>
> PROSPECT: Well, we estimate that we'll have to stop hiring new staff next year if we get another increase. <IMPACT>
>
> SALESPERSON: How will that affect your business?
>
> PROSPECT: We initially thought it would constrain our ability to support new customers. But we've automated aspects of the

onboarding process so we won't need as many people. So at this point, we think we can live with it.

SALESPERSON: Our customers have told us that a high-touch onboarding process delivers higher levels of customer satisfaction. Does moving to a low-touch model worry you at all?

PROSPECT: I hadn't thought about that, but you're probably right. We depend on customer satisfaction for a follow-on upsell. I guess there could be an issue there. <IMPACT>

SALESPERSON: If you had to put a dollar value on that, what would you guess?

PROSPECT: Well, about 30 percent of our revenues come from post-sale add-ons, so this could be significant—maybe as much as $500,000 per year. <QUANTIFIED IMPACT>

SALESPERSON: Okay, so you're telling me that if you don't fix this problem by year-end, you could see a revenue loss of around $500,000—is that correct? <RECAP>

PROSPECT: You're right—this could be a big deal. We really should get this solved as soon as possible. <QUANTIFIED IMPACT × URGENCY = IMPORTANCE>

In this example, the prospect didn't agree with the first suggested Impact, so the seller suggested a different one, which was more relevant to the prospect. Sometimes, you will need to make several suggestions before finding one that the prospect agrees is valid. To do this well requires the seller to have thought of some alternatives in advance. If the prospect doesn't buy into any of your suggestions, you then have two options. First, simply ask if the prospect sees any significant Impact if they don't resolve the identified Problem. Perhaps say something like, "Hey, it sounds like these escalating costs aren't a big deal for you or your company—have I got that right?" If they come up with some Impacts, explore each further, and try to quantify them. If not, it's time to move on! The Problem of increasing costs isn't perceived to be a big deal, at least at this point, so stop talking about it. Instead, look for other Problems that they might perceive as significant. The worst thing you can do is continue harping on about how you can address a particular Problem when they've made it clear to you that **they don't care.**

It's essential to ask about both Problems and their Importance for three reasons:

1. So that the prospect becomes more aware of the need to take action.

2. So that the prospect is prepared to explain and defend to others why the company needs to take action.

3. So the salesperson knows what features of their offerings (or company) to emphasize in their sales pitch. These are the ones that address Problems your prospect has explicitly stated as being important to solve.

Point 3 above is pretty important. Your odds of success in a Complex Sale increase if you can reduce a buying decision's complexity. You do this by focusing your message on just the critical few features that address the stated needs and ignoring the rest.

YOU ONLY HAVE SO MUCH AIRTIME WITH A PROSPECT. DON'T WASTE IT TALKING ABOUT FEATURES THAT ADDRESS PROBLEMS YOUR PROSPECT DOESN'T SEE AS IMPORTANT. IT TELLS THEM YOU WEREN'T LISTENING.

You also want to avoid the trap of assuming that a stated Problem is important to the prospect. As sellers, we will often hear a common Problem, like in the scenario above, and fail to ask about its Importance. Instead, we assume it's important and plan our selling strategy around it, only to find out later that no one thinks it's a big deal.

I assume to much!

Another error is putting down your shovel as soon as you've come across one small Problem that you can fix. Keep digging—your odds of winning a deal increase if you can find more. Changing suppliers is a hassle, and any new purchase comes with risks. So be sure you have enough critical gold nuggets to make the effort and cost worthwhile.

Often, a potential customer will ask you to quote before you fully understand their situation. Perhaps the prospect thinks they know what is needed and want to get on with it. Or they really aren't that interested in what you're selling, but if they ask you to go away and quote, you'll go away. And then they can ghost you. Resist the temptation. You should almost never put together a proposal unless the prospect has explicitly stated one or more Problems and why they are important to solve. If you do quote, you are no longer in a position to sell or motivate. Now, you might have noticed I said "almost never" versus "never" propose. There are situations when you might. For instance, when you think Clerking makes sense given the situation (check out the situations listed in Chapter 1). Responding to a Request for Proposal (RFP) is one situation where many sellers quote without understanding the Problems and their relative Importance. That's why the odds of winning one without having been deeply involved beforehand are right up there with winning the next lottery jackpot. As such, many savvy companies refuse to respond to RFPs unless they're the incumbent or have participated in writing it. In many cases, responding to an RFP is Clerking 101.

SORRY, WE DON'T SHARE THAT

Now, you might be wondering what to do if a prospect refuses to provide you with information about their Problems and Importance—information you need to sell and motivate. This can happen quite a bit, most often when you try to quantify the Impact. For example, asking about revenues, profit margins, costs, or other financial data often leads to the response, "Sorry, we don't share that information." Yet, when you're trying to understand the Impact of not resolving a particular Problem, these kinds of numbers are precious. If a buyer doesn't want to share this information, there are typically two reasons. First, they might sincerely believe the information is confidential, so they shouldn't share it with outsiders. Or they lack trust regarding your intentions with the information. They might think to themselves:

> Will you share it with others, or will you use it against me? Other sellers don't ask for this information, so why are you asking—something must be up, and I don't want you to take me for a fool.

For these situations, here are a few techniques you should try to help get the information you need.

SALES PLAYS: WIIFT, SHARE FIRST, AND BRACKETING

Let's say you want to know what a prospect is paying for a product or service that they currently buy from a competitor. When you ask, they tell you the information is confidential, and they don't give it to suppliers. The first thing to do is validate their objection. Tell them you understand why they might not want to share this information, and add that you hear this a lot from other clients. Avoid asking them WHY they won't share it, as asking WHY helps reinforce their position. Instead, simply say that you understand, and then try one of these Sales Plays.

WIIFT

Start by explaining why you need the information, and here is the critical part—the "why" must be a WIIFT (What's In It For *Them*) reason, not a WIIF-You. Reps often make the mistake of asking a prospect to do something and explain the rationale as it relates to benefiting themselves. Instead, you could say you want to do a quick cost analysis to see if you can save them some money and not waste their time if you can't. Or perhaps you could tell them you are looking for how they would benefit from working with you and thought this might be a good starting point. Either way, you have to give a plausible reason why it's in their best interest to share.

SHARE FIRST

In most relationships, you have to give something to get something. Selling is no different. So after explaining why a buyer should provide you with certain information, share what you know. Maybe share something like:

> Many of our customers tell us they pay between $X and $Y per widget from other suppliers. Is this what you're seeing?

OR

> We've heard that some suppliers have been offering super low prices on Product A but make up the difference by charging a higher price for Product B. Has this been your experience?

Often, by simply sharing what you know first, the prospect will become at ease because other companies are sharing this information. Also, this strategy can help elevate your relationship with the buyer, particularly with executives or subject-matter experts. You're now someone who brings valuable information instead of someone who just comes looking for it.

BRACKETING

If you've tried explaining and sharing and are still getting resistance, try a Bracketing strategy. Bracketing helps you get an estimate versus a precise number, which might be all you need at this point. Start by telling your prospect that you would like a rough idea to decide if this is worth pursuing further. Then ask about some possible ranges—maybe you would say:

So, is it roughly between $5 and $10 per pound, $10 and $15 per pound, $15 and $20 per pound, or more than $20?

Often, your buyer will respond with something like "the second one," and then you're done. Now you can use this as a guide to decide if this is a Problem you can address.

If none of these strategies work, it's time to start looking for other Problems where the prospect might be more open to sharing specifics. We'll explore the challenges of an uncooperative buyer further in Chapter 5.

Before we wrap up this chapter, let's answer one more question you might have. Is it ever okay to just tell? Sometimes—but it should always be your last resort. For example, say you're in a meeting, and you've asked your list of Fact and Problem questions but can't seem to find anything that the buyer might want to fix. You've even asked the "Hail Mary" question where you say, "Is there any part of your business you'd like to change where we could help?" and they respond with "No, not really." Then it's time just to tell. Briefly explain the problems or opportunities you help companies address and the benefits they achieve and offer that you would like to reconnect if they are ever in such situations. Occasionally, something will pop up on the spot, but more likely, you'll have to wait until a future relevant need arises.

KEY TAKEAWAYS

The first pillar in the P3 Selling method is "Problems," and I've put it first for a very good reason. It is the foundation of B2B selling upon which all else depends. Here are the critical concepts we discussed, along with a few Sales Plays, essential to your success.

Businesspeople don't buy products or services. They buy solutions that resolve problems or provide ways to capture new opportunities. So, until you have identified one or more Problems that a potential customer wants to address, you cannot sell. You can only Clerk!

Just because you've uncovered one or more Problems, there's no guarantee your prospect is going to do anything about them. Your job is to understand and influence how the prospect perceives each Problem and the Importance of resolving them. And you don't do this by telling them what they should see as important. You do it by asking questions that create and increase awareness around the Problem's Impact and Urgency. Whenever you hear a prospect state a Problem, you should be thinking, "So What?" and explore further. Remember that Fact questions enable you to quote, Problem questions enable you to sell, and questions about Importance enable you to motivate. So resist the temptation to put together a proposal as soon as you have enough Facts. Sometimes it works, but it's not selling—it's Clerking.

Besides influencing the need to take action, asking good Problem and Importance questions helps prepare prospects to defend their actions to others. It also guides you on which aspects of your product or company to emphasize in your proposal.

I also presented a few Sales Plays to help you get the information you need in order to sell and motivate, such as a credible WIIFT, Sharing First, and Bracketing to get a ballpark answer.

If none of these work, it's time to look for other Problems that might be less sensitive. If you can't find any Problems, put on your Clerking hat for a final try before moving on.

Spend some time on the activities below before moving to the next chapter, where we'll explore P3 Selling's second key element: People.

MAKE IT YOUR OWN

Sellers tend to ask a ton of Fact questions because they're easy once you have some basic product knowledge. But few of us are fast enough to come up with really good questions or suggestions about Problems, Impacts, and Urgency without some advanced planning. That's why I highly recommend taking the time to apply the concepts in this chapter to your selling situation by following these four steps:

1. Start by making a list of problems or opportunities that your products or services can address. Organize them by different market segments or buyer types if some won't apply to all. You will use this list to both ask and suggest during your sales calls.

2. Update your list of Fact questions. You probably have a list already that focuses on the information needed to develop a proposal. But you also need Fact questions that provide some clues on which of your Problem questions to ask. You will use these added questions as your roadmap, early in your call, on which direction to go.

3. Then, for each Problem on your list, document the potential

Impacts if a company doesn't address them. Keep asking "So What?" until you get to something highly motivating for someone to act. Also, be sure to consider both business and personal Impacts. As with your list of Problems, you will use these Impacts to both ask and suggest during your calls.

4. Lastly, make a list of questions you would ask or suggest to create more awareness around Urgency. They should help your prospect answer the question, "Why is this a priority for the company or for me to act now?" This category of questions and suggestions is often the most difficult for sellers. Try to avoid the typical suggestions that sellers artificially impose, such as "The sale price will only last until the end of the month." Even if true, they tend to erode the salesperson's credibility. Instead, think in terms of risk. What risks to the business, employees, customers, or the prospect themselves increase if they fail to take action? The more you can make it about them and not about you, the greater the trust you will establish.

As a final activity, think about where you are likely to get an objection when asking for needed information. For each situation, document a compelling WIIFT and something you might Share First to help overcome these objections.

objection = overcome w/ what is in it for them.

CHAPTER 3

P2: PEOPLE

Sports, politics, and buying decisions.
Everyone has an opinion.

Over the last decade, many respected firms have researched the B2B buying process. Organizations such as CSO Insights, TOPO/CEB/Gartner, *Harvard Business Review*, SiriusDecisions/Forrester Research, and Challenger, to name a few. Interestingly, they've all noticed the same phenomenon—the number of people involved in a company's buying decisions has been increasing. About ten years ago, many researchers found the average to be about five people. But five years later, that number jumped to around seven. We've recently seen the number increase again to ten or more people and sometimes as many as twenty. Wow—that's a whole lot of people weighing in on each purchase. And the size of these buying teams wasn't just for large, multibillion-dollar organizations either. One researcher reported that even companies with one hundred to five hundred employees had seven or more people involved in most buying decisions.

MORE PEOPLE, MORE PERSPECTIVES

Okay—now the scary part. Not long ago, research by Microsoft reported that 78 percent of sales professionals sell to only ONE person in accounts where they are trying to close a deal. ONE PERSON! And the research went on to report that only 7 percent of sellers sell to six or more people. This means that over 90 percent of salespeople only sell to half or fewer of their prospect's decision-makers. Now, if you remember back to our discussion on exploring Problems from Chapter 2, you should be thinking to yourself, "So What?" Good question—why is this important? Well, the same Microsoft study also reported that well-connected sellers had a 34 percent higher win-rate than those who only chatted up one person. Also, that same group had shorter sales cycles, so they got paid sooner and had more time to work on other deals.

Another risk factor to consider is turnover. Research conducted a few years back by LinkedIn showed that decision-maker turnover is increasing. It reported that "1 in 5 decision-makers (defined as those in 'director-level-and-above' roles) turns over every year."[1] So for every five deals, one decision-maker will likely be gone before your deal closes, unless you have short sales cycles or happen to be very lucky.

FOCUSING ALL YOUR SELLING EFFORTS ON A SINGLE PERSON IS AS RISKY AS PLACING ALL YOUR BETS ON A SINGLE ROULETTE NUMBER. BOTH STRATEGIES ARE ATTRACTIVE BECAUSE THEY'RE EASY, BUT NOBODY'S GETTING RICH FROM THEM.

That's why it's essential to identify, connect with, and influence as many decision-makers as possible. This brings us to the second pillar in the P3 Selling method: People.

The people you need to focus on fall into two categories:

1. People who are affected by the Problems (Problem People)

OR

2. People who play a role in the company's buying-decision process (Process People).

Often, people impacted by the Problems are also involved in the buying process, but not always. Let's start with the first group— the Problem People.

PROBLEM PEOPLE

As discussed earlier, until you've identified Problems that a prospect has agreed to try and solve, asking about who is involved in the decision makes little sense. That's because businesspeople don't buy products or services. They only buy ways to fix problems or capture opportunities. So the Problems define the decision-makers. Sure, you might reason that certain people have always made these kinds of purchase decisions, so why would this time be different. But if the company is looking to address some newly identified Problems, the decision-makers can undoubtedly change. Most commonly, the decision will now include people most impacted by the new Problems. Let me give you an example of this.

Let's say you are working with a prospect with your usual, but not always ideal, "We can save you money" pitch. Based on this value proposition, you might assume that whoever has P&L responsibility plus someone in finance would be the key decision-makers. But what if, unknown to you, the primary reason for replacing their current supplier was poor product or service reliability? This issue was causing a lot of customer dissatisfaction and costly turnover. So, in this case, perhaps the head of sales or customer service would want to get involved. And if they do, you can be sure that each of them will have different objectives that go beyond saving a few dollars. A seller who doesn't know this is going to miss the opportunity to address their needs. And if the competition figures it out and pitches a solution to these Problems, chances are good they're going to win the deal.

Also, repeat purchases or renewals often have different people involved in the buying decision versus the group that made the initial selection. And very likely, they will have different objectives. So if you don't know their goals (the problems or opportunities they're trying to address), you are at a significant disadvantage because "you do not know what you are selling!"

> *"I've learned that two people can look at the exact same thing and see something totally different."*
> —OMER WASHINGTON

So, your first task is to figure out who might be impacted by each Problem. After you've uncovered and perhaps raised the Importance of specific Problems, ask your contact whom these Problems might affect and why. Just knowing that Joe or Mary perceives a Problem as important isn't enough. Keep asking

"So What?" to yourself so you can get to the heart of the issues. Don't assume you know the answer or that it's obvious—ASK. Many sellers don't ask these second-level questions because they're afraid of looking stupid or just assume they know the answer. Instead, by probing deeper, your customer will see you as more of a consultant.

An easy way to do this is by stating the obvious and then exploring further. For example, you might say, "You mentioned that your head of marketing is very concerned about the uptime of your website. Is that because it creates a poor image to potential customers, or is it more than that?"

Sometimes, your contact won't know or be sure of the answer. Or worse, they might just take a guess. Capture what they tell you, but plan to validate it later—kind of a "trust everyone, but always cut the cards" approach. Prospects often guess, make assumptions, project their opinions onto others, or sometimes don't think it's that important for you to get it right. But it is imperative if you want to develop a winning proposal. Bear in mind that not everyone wants to solve a particular Problem, and they could interpret a solution as a threat for some reason. Helping one person capture an opportunity could create another person's problem. As such, be sure to ask about people who might have these negative perceptions since they could torpedo your deal.

PROCESS PEOPLE

The second category is people that play an expert role in the buying-decision process. Almost every company has a "standard" set of steps that are designed to keep them out of trouble when buying a product or service. I put the word "standard" in quotes because it often changes for reasons that aren't always predictable. While we'll explore these processes in more detail in the next chapter, for now, let's just make a list of the people who often take part in these steps. Process People tend to be subject-matter experts with deep knowledge or experience in some part of the buying process. Typical examples are those in finance, legal, regulatory, engineering, or IT who evaluate a buying decision based on their expertise. Generally, these people don't care about solving a particular Problem, unless it impacts them. Instead, their focus is on maintaining their expert credibility and stature regarding specific buying-decision criteria. As such, they will check to see whether a decision meets their legal standards, financial return on investment (ROI) standards, technical standards, etc. Fundamentally, their job is to ensure a particular decision step is "correctly" executed based on their perception of "correct." To find out who these people are, ask your contacts to tell you who else is likely to participate in the decision process beyond those impacted by the Problems. Take note of who they are, any information on where they focus, and their perceptions of "correct."

WHEN THE LIST IS LONG

Now, after a bit of research, you might find yourself with a long list of people—people you need to meet so you can understand, influence, and message to their perspectives. However, even though your chances of winning increase with each meeting, it won't be possible to connect with everyone at times. As such, I recommend you prioritize your list based on two factors:

1. Whether or not you expect a person to be part of the decision process. For example, excluding people impacted by a Problem (say, in the case of poor internet service) but not involved in the supplier-selection decision will help shorten your list.

2. A person's level of Decision Influence, which is a measure of how likely it is they will affect the final decision based on their Drive and Authority. Drive is related to a person's perception of a Problem OR a buying-decision criteria. If they see either of these as personally important, they are much more likely to get involved and try to influence the final decision. As for Authority, people acquire Authority within a company in two ways:
   A. Traditional Authority, which is acquired based on a person's title, position, seniority, level in the organization's hierarchy, or an official assignment. Presidents often have more authority than Vice Presidents, for example.
   B. Charismatic Authority, a concept developed by the sociologist Max Weber, which can be acquired in a variety of different ways. We've all come across people who have a lot of Authority even though they don't have impressive titles or formal decision-making roles. Perhaps they're a high performer or a recognized expert in a particular area. Maybe they've had a history of making successful recommendations or are very politically savvy. These people always seem knowledgeable about certain topics and often have relationships with those who have a high degree of Traditional Authority. And because of this, their opinions and ideas tend to inspire others to follow their recommendations.

Here's an easy way to estimate Decision Influence. If you think someone has a high degree of Authority, either Traditional or Charismatic, give them a score of 3. If they have moderate Authority, score them a 2, and low or no Authority scores a 1. Now do the same for Drive as it relates to the Problems identified or the buying-decision criteria. If the person views one or the other as highly important, give them a 3. Moderately important a 2, and not very important scores a 1. Adding the scores for Authority and Drive together gives you an estimate of their Decision Influence. The table below summarizes this scoring:

Decision Influence Rating Table	Authority Traditional or Charismatic	Drive Problem or Decision Criteria Importance
High	3	3
Moderate	2	2
Low	1	1

Using this table, here's an example of how you would calculate someone's Decision Influence:

A person with High Authority (3) + Moderate
Drive (2) = Has a Decision Influence of 5

Now take your list of people and split it into two—(1) those who are part of the decision process, and (2) those who are not. Start by prioritizing the first group based on their Decision Influence. Mark those with a Decision Influence score of 5 or greater as "must-meet" people. Ones who score 4 are also important to meet if at all possible. Target anyone with a score of 3 or below only if you have enough time and resources.

So what about those not part of the decision process—should you ignore these people? Not always. Here are a couple of situations where connecting with them makes good sense. For one, even if they aren't part of the decision process, people with a high degree of Decision Influence can be valuable to meet for two reasons. First, these people tend to get involved unexpectedly, so reaching out in advance can be a handy insurance policy. Second, you might want to encourage them to become involved in the decision, particularly if they have a positive view of you or your solution. Also, try not to ignore anyone who has a high degree of Drive, as they will often spend a great deal of energy trying to become part of the decision process. Even if they fail, they could sabotage your sale after the decision is made.

If you're unsure how to score each person, start by asking your key contacts what they think. Inquire about similar previous buying decisions—who got involved, who cared the most, and who had a great deal of influence. And try not to rely only on just one person's opinion. Ask others, both within the organization and even outside, if you think they might have a credible perspective. One significant consideration when gathering this information is a person's job or company tenure. The reliability of what they tell you will often correlate to how long they've been around. The longer, the more likely they've been through a few buying-decision cycles and will know "who's who in the zoo." If your primary contact is relatively new in their job or with the company, try to find another source for validation.

GETTING A CONVERSATION

Once you've prioritized everyone, you now have to get those critical meetings so you can understand and influence each of their perceptions. And in knowing their perceptions, you can put together a message that aligns to their needs and interests—and gets their support. Also, you reduce the risk of being blindsided by a need that comes out of left field—one that, if not addressed, could result in either a stalled or lost decision. If you understand, influence, and develop the right messaging for more people than your competitor, you'll have a much greater chance of winning the sale. And vice versa.

Now, in trying to arrange a conversation with these people, I'm sure you're aware that the old tactics of picking up the phone or firing off a catchy email don't work as well these days. And casually meeting up with them at an event or while wandering their office halls might allow you to put a face to the name but often won't win you the right to a proper sit-down where you can ask serious questions. So instead, try one of the following leading strategies.

AN INTRO

The best strategy is to get someone credible (either from inside or outside the company) to introduce you and request a meeting. But for them to do this requires some level of trust. Trust that you won't make them look like an idiot for introducing you, and trust that you won't use this introduction to undermine them. In addition to trust, sometimes your primary contact will object because of ego, as having you speak to others implies they aren't the only decision-maker—even when they aren't. So to make this strategy work, you're going to have to come up with a compelling reason. Back in the chapter on Problems, I suggested a couple of objection-handling Sales Plays. The first two are good ones to try here: WIIFT and Sharing First.

If you've done a great job of uncovering your contact's Problems and their perception of the Importance of addressing them, you are in an excellent position to frame your request. For example, a simple WIIFT request might be as follows:

> Given the Importance of resolving these Problems as soon as possible, it would be best if we could schedule short meetings with your boss and the head of finance. That way, we can uncover any unique requirements they might have so we can address them in our proposal. In addition, it would help us avoid any delays in getting your Problems fixed. Would you agree that this makes sense?

However, if you didn't do such a good job of uncovering Problems and their perceived Importance, you might not get much agreement when you make your pitch. Remember that understanding Problems enables you to sell, but understanding and raising awareness around Importance enables you to motivate. So if there's no motivation at this stage, then it's time to go back and revisit a Problems and Importance discussion. Don't worry about having to back up to get this critical information, as going forward without it puts you at risk of being ghosted without recourse.

Another way to deal with pushback is to first validate their objection and then try Sharing. Be sure you ASK afterward and not tell. For example:

> I understand your concern about involving your boss at this early stage. Other key decision-makers have expressed similar concerns that their boss is either too busy or doesn't like to meet with salespeople. But we've had quite a few situations where we didn't get executive (or finance, or regulatory, or...) input before developing our approach and got blindsided by a concern we hadn't considered. It made our key contact look really bad, and the project went on the backburner indefinitely. If we put together a meeting plan that you think they would find valuable, would that be a good approach?

You're also going to have to put them at ease that you won't make them look bad for organizing the meeting. Here you'll need to demonstrate that you know how to talk professionally and at the same level as the person you want to meet. To resolve this concern, explain exactly what you'll be talking about in the call. For Problem People, your goal is to understand their perceptions around Importance and any preconceived ideas on addressing them. For Process People, you want to learn about the specifics around their decision criteria so you are in the best possible position to comply. The key is to stress that you won't be talking about anything related to your product, features, or company beyond a very cursory overview unless requested. If you do, it might be your last intro to a meeting, either offered or accepted. Also, be careful of asking senior executives too many Fact questions, as most tire of them rapidly. Instead, share a few critical Facts that you've uncovered, and ask for their validation. Ideal Facts to confirm are high-level goals, objectives, or concerns versus getting into the minutiae around their current costs for widgets.

RELATIONSHIP MAPPING

Another meeting strategy is called Relationship Mapping, where you map individuals within your organization to people with corresponding levels or responsibilities in your prospect's account who play a role in the buying decision. For example, you might only map your boss to your contact's boss if the opportunity or account size is small. In more significant deals or larger organizations, the mapping should involve multiple departments and levels. Once mapped, you'll need a compelling WIIFT reason why each person should meet with someone from your team. Give your primary contacts advanced notice of this executive outreach and explain why it's essential. Again—make sure the rationale is a WIIFT and not about you.

SOCIAL MEDIA

A third strategy is to leverage social media platforms such as LinkedIn or Twitter. While a detailed discussion on using these sites is beyond the scope of this book, I will share some basics. First, before reaching out to people, you need to ensure you have created a credible profile that establishes you as someone worthy of a connection. Photos, taglines, and summaries that position you as a professional, consultative Problem solver are essential starting points.

Let's focus on LinkedIn for some examples of how you might do this. Instead of just listing your title, explain how you can help companies. For example, my LinkedIn profile headline doesn't list my job title as a sales consultant—it says:

> Strategies and best practices that help organizations transform their channel and direct sales teams from suppliers to trusted advisors.

Your "About" section should detail the kinds of customers you've worked with and the specific value you can bring. The key is to establish your credibility as someone who understands and has experience addressing relevant business problems and opportunities. Save the details about your company and product for the "Experience" section. Sellers looking to establish their consultative credentials further will periodically post articles or blogs on trends or other insights they think their customers will find of value. Avoid posting material that looks like an ad for your company or product. If that's all you have to share, it's best to stay silent.

Once you have a professional profile in place, be sure to send a connection request to every new contact you meet. I tend to do this after my initial meeting to thank them for their time. This way, your name will be top of mind, and you're much more likely to have your request accepted. After you have connections to one or more contacts within an account, it will be easier for you to find the other people on your "must-meet" list. When asking to connect with someone you've not met, always give a reason that is both personalized and in a WIIFT context. Most of the connection requests I receive either have no reason or one that is pretty lame, like, "Hey, noticed you're connected to Bob and Mary, so I thought it would be great for us to connect." Where's the WIIFT in that? Instead, maybe share that you're having discussions with their company about improving their widget manufacturing and wanted to connect just in case they wanted to learn more. Get creative, but always make it about them and not you.

Once you're connected, share any information you feel they might find interesting, but don't overdo it. And again—keep it at the right level, and no product or company advertisements. After developing some virtual rapport, you might reach out and ask them for a short meeting to get their perspectives or guidance on your project. Even if you don't get the meeting, the person is more likely to remember you in a positive light should your name come up during the buying process.

PRIMARY MEETING OBJECTIVES

Once you've arranged meetings with people on your target list, now's the time to plan how you'll achieve your primary objectives. There are three:

1. **Understand** each person's perceptions of the identified Problems, their Importance, and the related buying-decision criteria. It's also essential to understand if they have any preconceived ideas on how to solve the Problems.

2. **Influence** each person's perceptions of the Problems, their Importance, and the buying-decision criteria. You may also need to influence any preconceived solution ideas that don't align with your offerings. Unfortunately, many reps assume you can't change a person's perceptions, particularly regarding buying-decision criteria. This can be a costly mistake.

3. **Capture** each person's perceptions so you can highlight them in your proposal. If some of them put you at a competitive disadvantage, you'll want to develop a strategy on how best to respond. Engaging others for coaching, particularly those with a lot of Decision Influence, is a sound approach to help counter perspectives or criteria that put your deal at risk.

Certainly, you might have other meeting objectives—like uncovering additional Problems and their Importance, assessing the Decision Influence of others, or getting introductions to more people on your target list. But you should consider the three listed above as your bare minimum. Whatever objectives you decide on, be sure to plan each call in advance. Think through what to ask and suggest and what to explain should you get an objection. What you don't want to do is just show up and wing it. Reps that wing it almost always end up Clerking because it's the easiest and most natural thing to do. Instead, you are much more likely to achieve your objectives by using the Ask↔Suggest:Recap, or ASR, Sales Play I introduced in Chapter 1 and the objection-handling Sales Plays I introduced in Chapter 2.

If you are forced to map internal people that don't have the skills to achieve these three key objectives, you have two good options. The first is to ensure they are fully prepared by developing a detailed call plan and coaching them on using the ASR Sales Play. If you don't think this will work, then once they've established a relationship, have your internal person ask their counterpart if they would agree to a short call with you. If a meeting with you is the best approach, be sure to present the rationale in a WIIFT manner to avoid an objection.

IF YOU CAN'T GET A MEETING

Before we wrap up this chapter, we should discuss one more situation you will likely encounter—when you can't get a meeting with one or more of your target contacts, particularly those with high Decision Influence. Here are some thoughts:

- Try to meet with someone close to them. Maybe a direct report or a peer they interact with regularly that has some degree of Charismatic Authority, even if they don't have a personal interest in the Problems. Tell them about your concerns about not understanding the target contact's perceptions and how this could lead to a poor solution. If you can establish some business credibility with these people, they will likely provide valuable coaching on how best to proceed. They may even arrange for an introduction.

- If you've done a good job of asking and influencing others on the Importance of addressing the Problems, those people will be in a solid position to advocate on your behalf. So try to get them to influence the key players you can't get to. If you simply tell them why they need to change, they will be far less effective at doing this. Asking and then having them explain their rationale gets them to think through how they would explain it to others.

- The reality is that you often won't get to everyone—but the more you do, the better your odds of winning. As the self-development expert Brian Tracy said, "Success is a numbers game; there is a direct relationship between the number of things you try and your probability of ultimately succeeding."

KEY TAKEAWAYS

Our second pillar in the P3 Selling method is "People"—those individuals who are going to have some say on whether or not their company accepts your sales proposal. Your goals are to identify and meet with them so you can understand and influence their perspectives. This allows you to develop a targeted sales message designed to get their support. Here are four important considerations I outlined around achieving these goals.

More and more people are involved in corporate buying decisions, and each is likely to have a different perspective on what's important and what's not. But most salespeople focus their selling efforts on only one or two decision-makers, which is a high-risk practice. It's risky because they will base their proposals on a limited set of information, and they won't have the opportunity to influence those who might believe there are better options than theirs. Studies show that by connecting with more decision-makers, the odds of winning a deal increase, while the sales-cycle duration shortens. So to leverage the odds in your favor, try to get in front of as many decision-makers as possible.

You may need to make trade-offs on whom to meet, particularly in larger accounts involving many people. If so, you should prioritize them based on two factors: whether they are part of the buying-decision process and their degree of Decision Influence. You'll often include those with high Decision Influence even if they aren't part of the buying decision. That's because these people have a tendency to insert themselves into the process when you least expect it.

We also discussed three strategies to get meetings with those on your target list. Generally, the best option is an introduction from someone who has a good relationship with the person you're trying to meet. For them to do so requires solid WIIFTs—one for the person doing the introduction and another for the target person you want to meet with. You'll also need a high level of trust with the person introducing you—trust that the introduction won't reflect poorly on them. Other strategies include mapping others to key account contacts and leveraging social media. I also talked about some considerations if you simply can't get in front of certain people.

Always think through your objectives before any meeting so you can put together an effective call plan. When conducting the call, your primary objectives will always be to understand and influence Problem or decision-criteria perceptions. Understanding each individual's perceptions allows you to address them in your proposal or develop a strategy to mitigate those that put you at a disadvantage. Other objectives, such as uncovering additional Problems, assessing other people's Decision Influence, or getting introductions to others, also require planning, particularly in using the ASR and objection-handling Sales Plays.

Be sure to spend some time on the activities below before starting the next chapter, where we'll delve into P3 Selling's third key element: Processes.

MAKE IT YOUR OWN

It's easy to fall into the trap of selling to only one or two people, even though we know it's not in our best interests. To help expand the range of influence within your accounts, follow the steps below to create a planning sheet as a guide.

1. Make a list of all the people, by company role or title, who are often involved in making a buying decision for your products or services. If this list changes based on the product or market segment, create multiple lists and title them accordingly. If you don't come up with at least six people for each product or market situation, you're not trying very hard. Be sure to capture:
   A. People typically affected by the Problems (Problem People) AND
   B. People typically focused on the company's buying-decision process (Process People).

2. For each role or title that you've listed, make the following notes:
   A. For Problem People, what factors usually cause them to perceive a Problem as important? Put yourself in their shoes, and think, "So What?"
   B. For Process People, what decision criteria do they usually perceive as important?
   C. Which people tend to have the most amount of Decision Influence? Note that you are capturing the "typical" situation here, so you will always need to validate this for each opportunity. Internal politics can sway things considerably.

3. Then, for each role or title, make a list of various strategies you could use to get connected with them:
   A. What WIIFTs would most interest them to meet with you?

B. Whom might you ask for an introduction, and what is the WIIFT for them to do so? List as many options as you can.

C. Whom within your company might you map to people within a prospect's account?

4. Lastly, think about where you are likely to get an objection when asking for an introduction. Then, for each situation, document what you might Share to overcome these objections.

As a final activity, look at your LinkedIn or Twitter account, whichever you use to connect with other businesspeople, and ask yourself these questions:

- What image am I projecting? A product seller or a Problem solver? What changes could I make to project the image I want? *Complex vs. Simple sale*

- How consistently do I use these platforms to connect with decision-makers that I've met within my accounts?

- What WIIFTs could I use to connect with decision-makers whom I would like to meet?

CHAPTER 4

P3: PROCESSES

*"Would you tell me, please, which
way I ought to go from here?"*

"That depends a good deal on where you want to get to."

"I don't much care where—"

"Then it doesn't matter which way you go."

—AN EXCHANGE BETWEEN ALICE AND THE CHESHIRE
CAT, *ALICE IN WONDERLAND*, LEWIS CARROLL

If you haven't been involved in a sales cycle that just seemed weird, it's only a matter of time. It goes something like this. You were working with a prospect that told you about several Problems that were very important to solve. So you rushed back to the office and put together a proposal that was sure to result in a quick win. Then they started ghosting you. They didn't return any of your calls or emails, and the deal you forecast for the month seemed to evaporate. Then all of a sudden, it was on again. They wanted you to make some minor changes to your proposal and get it back right away. And when you did, once again, everything stopped. A few months later, you responded to another request, and then, more silence. You wondered what the heck was going on. It was like you were on a killer roller coaster that had no end to it. Maybe they eventually bought something from you or a competitor, or perhaps the opportunity just slowly faded away. Whatever happened, it consumed a ton of your time, diminished your credibility with management, and gave you a whole lot of stress and frustration along the way. So what the heck did happen? Very likely, you weren't in sync with their buying-decision process.

In the last two chapters, we talked about how selling depends on uncovering, influencing, and messaging around Problems to key people involved in a buying decision. If that were all you had to do, this book's title would be *P2 Selling*. However, there's a third factor—one that involves identifying, influencing, and aligning your selling activities to your prospect's buying-decision Process.

THE SELLING PROCESS MUST FOLLOW THE BUYING PROCESS, NOT THE OTHER WAY AROUND.

The buying-decision Process is the glue that connects Problems with People and results in Action. Without the Process, nothing happens. Here's a graphic that explains this relationship.

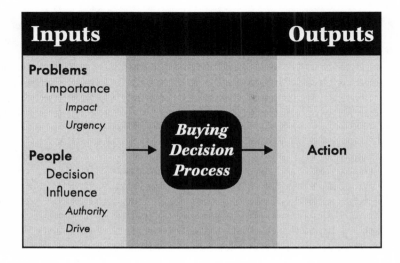

You may think that all you need to do is to ask your contact to explain their buying Process so you can follow along. Not quite. That's because there are actually TWO different buying Processes that require selling. There is a buying-decision Process that each individual goes through as well as one for the company. They are separate Processes but interconnected as it relates to getting a deal out of the other side. Let's look at these one at a time, starting with the individual buying-decision Process.

INDIVIDUAL BUYING-DECISION PROCESS

Researchers have studied the process individuals use to make buying decisions for quite a while. In 1910, the psychologist John Dewey documented the five stages of the buying-decision Process, which has been further researched and better understood over time. The basic idea is that people travel through five separate stages in succession to make a buying decision. These five stages are as follows:

1. **Need Recognition.** This stage is when something or someone has triggered an individual's awareness of a problem or opportunity. While creating awareness is fundamental to selling, often a person is already aware of a need before a salesperson gets involved.

2. **Information Search.** Here, a person starts searching for information around options to address the need. While in days of old this could have been a long and cumbersome process, today one can get information on almost anything with just a few mouse clicks. However, we continue to look to our friends and colleagues for their recommendations as well as our own past experiences.

3. **Evaluate Alternatives.** This stage is where a person starts assessing various options on how well they believe each will solve a Problem. This process is often more of a "gut-feel" analysis than anything formal or structured. It's also heavily influenced by any emotional attachments, positive or negative, that someone might have toward the alternatives.

4. **Purchase Decision.** Here is where an individual decides on the "whether" to buy and the "what" to buy. At the end of this stage, the person will take some form of action that completes the purchase, move the buying Process forward, or simply decide to do nothing.

5. **Post-Purchase Evaluation.** The last stage is where an individual evaluates whether the purchase adequately resolved their needs. Fundamentally, they ask themselves, "Did I make the best decision?" We won't spend much time here

beyond pointing out that this is a critical stage to manage if your company depends on repeat sales or provides a subscription-based service.

While we have access to more tools, technologies, and information to support our decisions today, the Process hasn't changed much since Dewey first introduced it. It's interesting to note that if someone perceives a particular buying decision as not very complex and low risk, they can progress through these five stages very quickly—often in a matter of minutes or seconds. Let me give you an example of each stage, in order:

1. You are in the checkout line at a grocery store and start feeling a little hungry. Your partner is preparing a big meal that you'll have in a few hours, so you don't want to overeat. (Need Recognition)

2. You see a display stand next to you that offers several snacks for sale. Some are larger than others, some sweet and others salty. You pick up a few of the packages and look for their calorie counts per serving. (Information Search)

3. Based on this information, you decide you might like a sweet snack if it contains fewer than one hundred calories. You also remembered a few previous choices you didn't enjoy, so you want to avoid them. (Evaluate Alternatives)

4. You find one snack that appears to check all the boxes, so you toss it in your cart and proceed to the checkout desk to pay for it. (Purchase Decision)

5. After finishing, you found your choice wasn't too filling and

tasted pretty good. You decide that you'll likely buy it again. (Post-Purchase Evaluation)

Over the years, researchers have studied this Process further to give more insights into how people progress through the stages. The first insight was that people tend to make better purchase decisions when spending more time in the early stages, defining their Problems and searching for information. "Better decisions" meant their selection was more likely to have done well in solving their Problems, and they experienced less "buyer's remorse" in Stage 5. They were also much more confident in making their final choice during the Purchase Decision stage.

Another finding was that when buying decisions were perceived as complex or risky, and there was considerable personal ownership in the outcome, individuals would force themselves to spend more time during these early stages. Studies have shown that people in these situations would consider more products, vendors, features, and information sources before moving on. As a result, decisions took much longer.

Other valuable observations were in the Purchase Decision stage. For many, there is quite a bit of stress associated with it, and people don't like to remain there for very long. Because of this, individuals want to make their final decision as quickly as possible, then take action, move back to an earlier stage if they lack confidence, or put the entire decision on hold. Two situations tend to cause a buying decision to stall during this stage. The first is if someone receives negative input from a credible friend or peer regarding their planned selection. The second is when some unforeseen event occurs, such as an organizational change, unexpected financial results, or other surprises. These last-minute situations can unnerve the decision-maker, causing them to delay or abandon the purchase. Even unexpected personal events or turmoil on the home front can have a similar effect. So for risky or complex decisions, individuals must have a high degree of confidence in their selection to avoid being distracted.

What does all this mean when your offerings address complex Problems that involve some degree of risk? It means your selling strategies need to support and align with an individual's decision Process and not conflict with it. Let me give you an example of what not to do using a typical Clerking "sales" pitch:

- "It would be great if your company were to buy one of our highly advanced widgets." (Stage 4: Purchase Decision)

- "Compared to other widget manufacturers, ours provide better price performance and higher reliability. We also have a special promotion going on this month that no one else is offering." (Stage 3: Evaluate Alternatives)

- "Let me share some information on our specs, industry reviews, and references from other clients who have installed them." (Stage 2: Information Search)

- "Would you see the value in having a closer look at these for your organization?" (Stage 1: Need Recognition)

The above Clerking pitch doesn't work well because it forces a prospective buyer to think in the exact opposite direction from how they naturally process information and arrive at a good, confident buying decision. Yet this approach happens all too often.

INDIVIDUAL PROCESS STRATEGIES

There are five essential strategies that you should use to help prospects successfully navigate their individual buying-decision Process. These increase the chances that the buyer selects your offerings during the Purchase Decision stage. They are as follows:

SPEND MORE TIME IN STAGE 1: NEED RECOGNITION

As discussed in Chapter 2, we often rush through this stage, which increases the risk of a stalled decision. We find one Problem, think we've hit the jackpot, and run off to put together a proposal. Instead, try to uncover and suggest as many problems or opportunities as you can. Then explore how the prospect will be affected if these were left unaddressed, both business-wise and personally. Finally, be sure to ask and suggest reasons why resolving each Problem should be considered urgent (Ask ↔ Suggest:Recap).

DON'T JUMP FROM NEED RECOGNITION TO PROPOSAL

Your prospect will go through the Information Search and Evaluate Alternatives stages with you or without you. You have a better chance of winning your deal if you go through these stages with them so you can create awareness in areas that they may not have considered. After summarizing their needs, help them transition to the Information Search stage by asking questions like:

- "So what kind of information would you need to create a good list of options?"

- "What have you done in the past?"

- "What kind of research would your boss or others expect you to have done before developing your selection criteria?"

- "How can I help you pull this all together?"

After your prospect has reviewed a good bit of information and they are satisfied they have all they need, help them transition to the Evaluate Alternatives stage by asking questions such as:

- "What criteria do you think are the most important in evaluating your options?"

- "What have you used in the past?"

- "How do we ensure your selection does the best job of addressing the Problems you identified?"

If your prospect doesn't have answers to these, now is a good time to suggest a few and ask if they would agree. Remember that alternatives don't have to include your competitors unless your prospect insists or if you think others might. One way to make people feel comfortable they have covered this stage is by suggesting options related to your solution. Perhaps ask a question like, "Would you find it valuable to explore the various options we have about implementing our solution?"

Ask about which products, features, or implementation would

work best. All are sound ways of increasing your prospect's level of confidence that they have done a proper job here. Remember, when selling in these stages, be sure to use the ASR Sales Play to influence by creating awareness.

ALIGN PROPOSALS AND SOLUTION PITCHES TO THE BUYING-DECISION PROCESS

Usually, you'll submit a proposal for consideration during the Evaluate Alternatives stage, after you've understood and influenced the decision criteria. Many proposals start by describing the supplier's company and then jump right into product features and pricing. Not ideal! If you followed the above strategies, you know quite a bit: you have a deep understanding of the Problems, information reviewed, and evaluation criteria. And there's a good chance you know this better than your competitors. So be sure to leverage it.

All proposals should start with a clear description of the prospect's stated Problems, who or what is affected, and why solving them is both important and urgent. Follow this with information about your solution that is directly relevant to their specific Problems, ideally from multiple sources—your company, customers, analysts, etc. Finally, explain how your recommended approach differentiates from other alternatives and best meets their decision criteria. This is where you would explain how great your company is, not upfront. Presenting in this manner reinforces and validates the natural decision process that your buyer takes and distinguishes you as a consultant versus just another clerk. It's also helpful to those seeing your recommendation for the first time, as the flow makes it easier to understand the reasoning behind it.

THE PURCHASE DECISION STAGE IS THE DANGER ZONE

We call this stage the "Danger Zone" because here, it's very easy for a deal to go south on you without much warning. As a result, here is some advice. The first is to do your best to ensure your key contacts have a high degree of decision confidence before they enter this stage. If you suspect there's a fair bit of hesitation, don't try to do a hard close. Instead, encourage them to move back a stage or two so you can help uncover what is putting them at unease and collaboratively solve for it. Perhaps they haven't defined the Problem and its Importance sufficiently, done enough research, evaluated enough options, or documented clear decision criteria. Whatever the reason for doubt, now is the time for you to help them address it.

Once they've gained confidence, encourage them to move back to the Purchase Decision stage. Then, you need to move quickly to tie up any loose ends so you can complete the sale. The thing you absolutely don't want to do, to use a highly technical term, is "fart around." The longer you're in this stage, the greater the risk that some unforeseen event will crop up or some well-meaning acquaintance will chime in with their opinion, and your deal becomes toast.

ALL PROBLEM PEOPLE TAKE THE SAME JOURNEY

Everyone impacted by the Problems needs to go through the same stages to feel comfortable with the decision. Depending on their level of personal ownership and perceptions of complexity and risk, they can move through the stages in a few minutes, a few months, or even longer. For example, a senior executive with a great deal of confidence in their subordinates can move through the stages quite quickly, particularly if presented with recommendations in a way that aligns with their buying-decision Process. So every time you meet with someone, be sure to assess which stage they are in so you can guide and support them in their journey. And if you aren't able to meet with some, be sure that your proposal lines up with the Process so they can easily follow the logic.

Two final comments on navigating the buying-decision Process: First, in most cases, you will not move someone through all of the first four stages during a single call, unless perhaps you're selling snacks. Sometimes, just getting through the Need Recognition stage will take multiple meetings, so don't move on until you're confident that your prospect is ready. Second, don't hesitate to encourage your prospect to move back a stage or two if you think they haven't spent enough time to develop sufficient awareness or confidence. Sometimes, you'll find a buyer in a late decision stage when you first connect with them, which means you've not had the opportunity to understand or create awareness in areas essential to your success. In these cases, ask the prospect if they would mind moving back so you can better understand their thinking. It's always better for a deal to take a bit longer than for it not to happen at all.

CORPORATE BUYING-DECISION PROCESS

Now let's turn our attention to the second Process you'll need to sell to—the Corporate Buying-Decision Process. Depending on the company and what they are buying, the buying-decision Process can vary wildly. In fact, it can change quite a bit from time to time, even when the same company is making the exact same buying decision. As such, always think of the typical steps as a guideline versus a strict rule of what will happen. Using the graphic illustrating the generic Process below, let's explain areas of complexity and the corresponding key selling strategies.

THE INITIATOR

The first thing to notice in the diagram above is the addition of an Initiator. This is a person or group that kicks off, or initiates, the buying-decision Process. These people or groups tend to have high Traditional or Charismatic Authority and enjoy driving change for whatever reason. They might be motivated to solve the Problems, or they might just get a kick out of taking the lead on someone else's cause. Also, they may or may not take part in the buying Process. Either way, they have the skills and relationships to get the right people together to start the Process. Asking which people or groups have initiated past buying decisions can provide valuable insights if your main contact has difficulty getting things started.

DECISION STREAMS

The standard corporate buying-decision Process looks a lot like the individual Process but more formal. The main difference is that there are two separate but interconnected decision streams that drive and govern the steps—the Consensus Stream and the Compliance Stream.

Consensus Stream

The Consensus Stream is where Problem People collaborate to move a buying decision forward. These are the people who perceive the Problems as important AND have a high degree of Decision Influence. We call it the Consensus Stream because to move the decision forward, participants need to reach some level of consensus around each step's outputs. For example, they need to agree on the Problems, why the company should solve them, which options decision-makers should consider, and what selection criteria they will use. However, getting consensus doesn't mean that everyone has to agree. Typically, a small number of people with the highest Decision Influence tend to define each step's outputs (remember that Decision Influence is a combination of Authority and Drive). Within this Stream, your goal is to get a critical mass of people through their individual decision Process so they'll influence others to support their thinking.

Some selling methodologies make a point of defining one of these people as "The Guy" (the noun "Guy" being gender-neutral). You may have heard terms such as the key decision-maker, decider, economic buyer, top person, or some other moniker. These labels imply that one person can override everyone else when making the final buying decision. These methodologies also tend to assign a persona to this person regarding their decision drivers, usually around core company financials like ROI, risk reduction, or growth. My opinion is that these characterizations are dangerous for three reasons.

The first is that in today's corporate environment, almost no competent leader will decide unilaterally over the objections of all others. Perhaps they did fifty years ago when many of these methodologies were created, but they rarely would today. Most senior executives will almost always trust their key people's perspectives and their company's decision Process. The characterizations can also be risky because they imply that the pitch to these people is always about core financials. They are important for sure, but everyone has different reasons for wanting a particular buying decision, and more often than not, it's at a personal level. I remember a sales situation where one decision influencer drove the buying Process simply because a particular Problem overwhelmed them each day with stress. The seller that focused their message on ROI and growth lost the deal. My last concern is that it suggests all a seller needs to do is get an audience with "The Guy," and they'll win the deal. However, we know from the stats shared in the last chapter that this simply isn't true.

Compliance Stream

We refer to the second stream as the Compliance Stream. Here is where the company has established buying-decision "rules" to protect itself from making poor decisions. These rules consist of policies, procedures, and criteria that define how to conduct each Process step. For example, during the initial Need Recognition step, the company might have established a minimum ROI before prioritizing a project for further consideration. In the Information Search step, there might be a requirement to consider at least three different vendors. And the Evaluate Alternatives step might specify using a formal RFP process for purchases above a set dollar amount.

The people within this stream are the company's subject-matter experts from areas such as finance, legal, regulatory, or IT. They are assigned the tasks of creating and overseeing the company's policies and procedures. As discussed earlier, a seller's objective throughout this Stream is to understand, influence, and comply with these policies when it makes sense. I say "when it makes sense" because at times you might not be able to or it's not in your best interest to do so. In such cases, you'll need to adopt a different approach, which we'll discuss a bit later. Also, you might find that some people are in both streams, which means you'll need to understand and influence them from a Problem-Importance and a Process-compliance perspective.

An important thing about the Compliance Stream is that the more a company perceives the buying decision as complex or risky, the more scrutiny will be around each step. For example, in my days working for Xerox, I always marveled at how relatively junior-level administrative people could make million-dollar (or more) decisions to buy copiers. But when buying computer hardware and software, many decisions a tenth of the size had to involve the most senior executives for approval. Companies saw buying copiers, a well understood and not very complex product from a reputable vendor whom they had purchased from before, as a not very risky decision. On the other hand, when buying relatively new computer printing technology that could put them out of business if it failed, the risk of making a mistake could be catastrophic.

Recently, a few things have changed within this Stream. The first significant change is that companies have easy access to much more information than they ever used to have. Vendor websites, analyst recommendations, customer reviews, blogs, and social media conversations are all just a few clicks away. As a result, many companies conduct buying decisions in an environment of information overload. TrustRadius, a product-review site, reported in a recent survey that "the average buyer uses 6.9 information sources to make a purchase decision,"[2] and that number is increasing—up to over 35 percent year over year between 2020 and 2021. Consequently, companies spend a lot more time analyzing information, which explains why the average corporate buying cycle takes substantially longer. The same TrustRadius survey reported the following data on B2B buyers for 2021 compared to before the pandemic:[3]

- 33 percent spend more time researching products

- 31 percent spend more time prioritizing selection criteria

- 33 percent spend more time comparing products

- 34 percent spend more time defining expected ROI

This vast amount of easily accessible information is making buying decisions much more complicated. This is one of the reasons we're seeing more and more people involved in the Process, something we pointed out in an earlier chapter. Gartner, another respected research firm, recently reported that 77 percent of B2B buyers stated that their "latest purchase was very complex or difficult."[4] So while many sellers feel that the selling Process is much more complicated than it used to be, it's essential to realize that the buying Process has also become more complex. As a result, many companies struggle with it. And for today's salesperson to remain relevant, a change in role is required. Traditionally, sellers were a buyer's key source of product information—no more. Today, all kinds of independent supplier information are easy to access and often considered more trustworthy. And it's not just credibility—companies also find accessing information without a seller involved to be more efficient. Many salespeople aren't even engaged until a company is halfway to two-thirds through a buying cycle, and then only to get some last-minute information that they can't find online.

CORPORATE PROCESS STRATEGIES

With these observations in mind, here are the top strategies to help you navigate the Corporate Buying-Decision Process and maximize your chances of a win.

LOOK FOR INITIATORS

Every Corporate Buying-Decision Process starts somewhere, and it often begins with a particular person or group that inspired others to act. You can find these Initiators by asking about past projects—how did they get started, who championed them, where did the "spark" come from that got the ball rolling? Often, these people are at the source of many different projects— think of them as "serial Initiators." Finding and engaging these people can make a big difference in gaining others' support. When reaching out, tell them that you are looking for their advice or guidance on starting or moving a buying Process forward. They often won't just guide you but will take an active role in making things happen.

SELL TO BOTH THE CONSENSUS AND COMPLIANCE STREAMS

Too often, sellers focus on a small number of people within the Consensus Stream and take whatever policies or criteria come their way from the Compliance Stream. A more successful strategy would be to connect with as many people as possible within both streams. Remember that actual selling involves understanding and influencing perspectives while developing messaging that aligns. Within the Compliance Stream, it's vital to understand the decision policies and criteria as early as possible to know if there are some that you can't meet or put you at a competitive disadvantage. Learning early in a deal that there are challenging conditions gives you time to do something about them. Finding out late in the Process can leave you with nowhere to go.

WHEN YOU CAN'T COMPLY

So what should you do if one or more established policies either put you at a disadvantage or are impossible for you to meet? For example, perhaps the legal team specifies that you must use their standard contract, which you know your company won't accept. Maybe the CFO states that price is the primary deciding factor, or their IT group decides that any new systems must have at least five customer references. If you know that some of these will be a challenge, you should first try influencing the appropriate subject-matter expert. Share stories and provide real-life examples to create awareness that they should alter their criteria for this particular purchase and then ask if they would agree. But never tell!

✗ TELLING ISN'T THAT EFFECTIVE WHEN IT COMES TO CREATING AWARENESS. AND IT TENDS TO PISS PEOPLE OFF, PARTICULARLY SUBJECT-MATTER EXPERTS WHO HAVE THEIR "EXPERT" STATUS TO MAINTAIN.

Instead of telling, validate, suggest, explain, and then ask. Here's an example of what a seller's dialogue might sound like:

> SALESPERSON: Thanks for sharing your selection criteria. I can fully appreciate why you want three or more customer references from your industry (Validate). Other customers had similar criteria but decided that because the technology was new to their industry but very well established in others, it would be better to consider additional industry references (Suggest). Otherwise, their business could get forced into selecting an older technology that they would have to live with for some time (Explain). Would you see value in expanding this qualification to consider a solution that is best suited to meet your company's current and future needs (Ask)?

This strategy won't always work, as the expert will often be much more knowledgeable on their topic area than you are and will stand their ground. If so, you have two choices—cross your fingers and hope OR reach out to Problem People in the Consensus Stream and enlist their help in changing the specs. Many reps take the first option, but my advice is to choose the second to improve your chances of winning. Schedule a call with one or more people with high Decision Influence that are supportive of your solution. Explain the risks to them corporately and personally if their company uses the current criteria.

As before, share stories and provide real-life examples to create awareness that they should alter their policy for this particular purchase. Companies create compliance criteria to protect and benefit their business, so showing that they fail to do this in this specific instance is the key to changing it.

ALIGN SELLING ACTIVITIES TO THE DECISION PROCESS

Remember that the buying Process is the decision-maker, so it's essential to assess its stage regularly so you can respond appropriately. For example, presenting a proposal before there's consensus around the need to solve a Problem or suggesting new Problems or selection criteria at the eleventh hour undermines a seller's credibility. Instead, your strategy should be to align your selling activities with the needs of the buying Process, not the other way around. Also, because the Process we've described is a general guideline, you'll need to check each sales opportunity for any unique variations.

In some cases, your primary contact might tell you that they are the sole decision-maker, and therefore, you should only work with them. To deal with this risky situation, start by **Validating** their assertion. Then you might **Explain** that you've worked with other sole decision-makers but have found that others often get involved at the last minute. Sometimes, they check the decision for compliance or weigh in on whether solving the Problems is necessary. This can slow things down, forcing the "decision-maker" to live with their Problems much longer than they want to. Then **Suggest** it might be better to connect with these people up-front to avoid any surprises. Finally, **Ask** if they would agree. If you've given a few good WIIFT rationales on why they should support this, you stand a reasonable chance of getting some meetings.

⚡ SIMPLIFY THE DECISION PROCESS

The fact is, confused prospects don't buy, yet today's corporate buying Processes often generate more confusion than answers. Sellers often contribute to the confusion by overloading prospects with too much generalized information about product features, industry awards, and white papers, along with proposals that contain way too many options. Sellers think that they're being helpful by giving buyers as much information as possible. However, as the psychologist Barry Schwartz explained in his book *The Paradox of Choice*, too much choice and complexity lead people to feel powerless and frustrated, resulting in a no-decision or increased buyer's remorse. Instead, try to make the buying Process easier by providing information that is clearly focused on solving specific, agreed-upon Problems. Information not directly related to specific Problems or compliance criteria unnecessarily complicates things.

POINTING OUT THAT YOUR COMPANY HAS WON BEST PLACE TO WORK FOR THE FIFTH YEAR IN A ROW IS GREAT INFORMATION IF YOUR PROSPECT NEEDS A JOB—NOT SO MUCH IF THEY ARE TRYING TO RESOLVE THEIR PRODUCTION ISSUES.

Buyer research reported separately by CEB and Gartner showed that sales-rep-information overload significantly reduced the ease of making a purchase and increased buyer's remorse or regret by 50 percent. Conversely, prescriptive information that helped guide the decision Process increased purchase ease dramatically and reduced buyer regret by over a third.

CHANGE YOUR ROLE

Ask yourself this question: in your prospect's mind, what should be your primary role as it relates to supporting their buying-decision Process? Some sellers tell me it's to be their company's expert on their offerings or the person who manages the relationship between the two organizations. My recommendation is that these should be secondary. To maximize your chances of winning a deal:

A SELLER'S PRIMARY ROLE SHOULD BE TO ACT AS THE EXPERT ON THE BUYING-DECISION PROCESS FOR THEIR SPECIFIC OFFERINGS.

You should think of yourself as a guide who advises the prospect on how best to navigate both the Consensus and Compliance Streams. In the Consensus Stream, you should be an expert on the Problems you typically solve, why they are important, and whom they tend to impact. You should advise on credible information sources, options to explore, and criteria to reach the best decision. You should know who will likely get involved in the Compliance Stream so you can encourage your contacts to bring these people in early. Then let them know what to expect and what questions will be asked, and collaboratively develop a plan to remove roadblocks and keep the Process moving. To be effective in this advisory role, you'll need to rely heavily on asking and suggesting.

KEY TAKEAWAYS

The third pillar in the P3 Selling method is Processes, which are the steps that both companies and people go through to make buying decisions. Successful selling strategies involve proactively identifying and influencing these Processes while ensuring that all sales activities are aligned. Here is a summary of the key insights I presented with regard to navigating these Processes.

The most important concept is that the buying-decision Process is the decision-maker—it acts as the framework that links Problems and People with Action. There are two different decision Processes: one that individuals go through and a second that the company has defined. Successful sellers must navigate and sell to both.

The individual Process starts when a prospect first recognizes a problem or opportunity and continues until they decide whether to resolve it. Time spent in earlier stages is essential, particularly when Problems are perceived to be complex or risky. Spending extra time here increases an individual's confidence as they approach a final buying decision. All Problem People need to go through each stage, so it's wise to avoid proposing a solution or asking for a purchase decision too soon. Sellers should structure all proposals or sales presentations to align with this decision Process.

The Corporate Buying-Decision Process is similar to the individual Process, but it has two interconnected and parallel streams—the Consensus Stream and the Compliance Stream. The Consensus Stream is driven by Problem People and dominated by those with a high degree of Decision Influence. The Compliance Stream consists of subject-matter experts who review buying decisions against policies and criteria designed to reduce risk. People in both streams will scrutinize decisions more closely as their perceptions of complexity and risk increase. Unfortunately, easy access to an almost endless supply of product and supplier information has made buying decisions much more confusing than ever before. Sellers should avoid contributing to this situation by providing information laser-focused on solving the prospect's Problems and conforming to the compliance criteria.

Lastly, to maximize the odds of winning, a seller's primary role needs to change from a supplier of product information to an advisor on navigating the decision Process. By offering guidance, anticipating each person's needs, and working collaboratively to remove obstacles, sellers can elevate their relationship and help prospects move through the decision Process faster, easier, and with less buyer's remorse.

In the next chapter, I'll present the P3 Selling Playbook, which details the most critical sales Processes you need for success. Before moving on, be sure to complete the activities below to personalize your Process selling strategies.

MAKE IT YOUR OWN

To become a buying Process expert, start by documenting the typical steps that a potential customer performs to make a buying decision for your products. If you are new to your company, enlist the help of your manager or co-workers who have more experience. Afterwards, make notes on the following:

- What additional Process details can you add?

- For the Corporate Buying-Decision Process, which people tend to get involved within each step, and when do they get involved—what triggers this? What activities do they perform once they get involved?
- For both the individual and corporate decision Processes, what information do people typically want to see and from which sources? How many different sources are generally required?
- For both decision Processes, what options are typically considered, and how differentiated are your offerings from these? Think at both the personal- and business-benefit levels.
- For the Corporate Buying-Decision Process, what are the typical policies and criteria used within the Compliance Stream? Who uses them, and what is the rationale for each?

- What obstacles are you or your prospect likely to encounter throughout the buying Process?
  - Do prospects have difficulty gaining consensus on a specific Problem's Importance, deciding on which information to use, or agreeing on the most appropriate selection criteria?
  - Which policies or decision criteria play in your favor, and what could you suggest to encourage prospects to include them?
  - What policies or decision criteria are often not in your favor? What credible explanations could you suggest that would justify changing them?

- What can you do to make the Process easier?
  - How could you enable greater collaboration throughout the Consensus Stream? Perhaps a workshop, a survey, or some other method to get everyone on the same page?
  - What information could you provide to help your prospects make faster or better decisions? When would the best time to provide this be and to whom?
  - What tools or resources could you provide your prospects that would simplify aspects of the decision Process? Perhaps streamlining the Problem definition, gathering information, or comparing options, especially if competitive differentiation is difficult. These should be supplier agnostic for credibility purposes, meaning they appear fair and don't obviously suggest a decision in your favor.
  - If your prospects regularly use an RFP Process, what boilerplate could you give them to make it easier to develop, deploy, and assess the submissions?
  - What suggestions could you make to avoid last-minute surprises? Perhaps bring in certain people earlier, offer to perform research or analysis, or conduct a brainstorming session around implementation options? Whom should these suggestions be made to, and at what stage?

Finally, look at your standard proposal templates and make sure they align with how people make buying decisions, not how a clerk talks about their products.

CHAPTER 5

P3 SELLING PLAYBOOK

"If you can't describe what you are doing as a process, you don't know what you're doing."

—W. EDWARDS DEMING

Let's be honest: consistent success in selling isn't easy, and applying the P3 Selling strategies doesn't come naturally either. While almost any seller can have a good month from time to time, only a few do it every month and every year. You know this to be true, or you wouldn't have taken the time to read this book. Zig Ziglar, the famous motivational speaker, used to say, "Sales is the highest paying hard work and the lowest paying easy work there is." The easy part, which we call "Clerking," generally doesn't pay very well. But the hard part, which involves creating awareness around a buyer's Problems, People, and Processes, certainly can, which is why many aspire to be great at it.

SELLING SUCCESS FACTORS

In my experience, there are three factors in achieving consistent selling success: skills, activity, and process. Think of these as the three legs of a stool: if any one of these is missing or weak, the stool falls over. Skills are about one's ability to perform specific selling tactics or Sales Plays—such as asking good questions, suggesting alternatives, presenting information, listening to understand, and responding to objections. Most people learn good selling skills by watching others, while some discover them through formal sales training. Either way, the only way to get good at them is through constant practice. Activity is about how often the seller performs these tactics. For example, someone with excellent questioning skills won't do very well if they only call on one customer per week. In Simple Sales situations, a person's activity level (their number of calls, emails, proposals, etc.) is a primary predictor of success. It's still essential in Complex Sales but much less of a performance guarantee, as quality tends to reign over quantity. The third factor is process. Just as companies have buying-decision Processes to protect them from risks, successful sellers use sales processes in complex B2B selling situations to avoid mistakes and achieve consistent results.

SELLERS WITH SOLID SKILLS AND ACTIVITY OFTEN EXPERIENCE INCONSISTENT RESULTS WHEN THEY FAIL TO REGULARLY FOLLOW A PROCESS.

To support this need, many companies document a collection of best practices, or a playbook, to guide sellers on the most effective way to manage their overall business. Playbook processes aren't just about helping you have a great sales call or winning a big deal. They're also about managing the big picture so you can make your quota month after month and year after year.

While playbooks can contain a wide range of processes, policies, procedures, tools, and resources, the P3 Selling Playbook focuses on just four of the most critical sales processes—ones that you need to know and regularly use to be successful:

- Prospecting

- Call Management

- Opportunity Management

- Pipeline Management

PROSPECTING

You may have experienced a feeling of dread when you saw the word "prospecting." If you did, you're not alone, as most sellers try to avoid both the word and the activity as much as possible. But few of us are likely to make our sales goals without it. Prospecting, at its core, is about two things: creating initial interest around problems or opportunities AND qualifying a contact regarding their interest and ability to address them. I like to think of prospecting as asking someone to dance. After presenting yourself as "the opportunity," you ask two questions in either order—are you interested in dancing, and are you able to dance? If the answer is yes to both of these, you can start dancing, which is a metaphor for selling. If you get a no to either question, move on to the next person in line and start again. The key is to raise just enough interest for someone to want to invest their time and energy to engage further. Talking about your "product" at this point tends to turn people off. I use the dancing analogy because it drives home the point that you need both parties engaged for selling to work.

There are many ways to do prospecting these days. Marketing departments initiate much of it through webinars, trade shows, email blasts, thought leadership, and other techniques that draw prospects to your website or cause them to reach out. And then, of course, there is the dreaded cold call. A cold call is when you reach out to a prospect who has no real relationship with you or your company by phone, mail, email, or social media. A warm call is to someone who has had some recent contact with you or your company and expressed at least a cursory interest in what you do. There are certainly some advantages to cold calls: they are simple, easy to implement, and provide fast feedback. They tend to work better with baby boomers over those who are more internet or social media savvy. They also have a higher success rate when using very targeted messages made to pre-qualified prospects. Conducting advanced research on titles, responsibilities, and potential needs and using this to craft a tailored message is key to getting results. As such:

SUCCESSFUL COLD CALLING REQUIRES TAILORED MESSAGING OR COMPLEMENTARY ACTIVITIES THAT WARM UP PROSPECTS BEFORE REACHING OUT.

The best way to warm up a prospect is to provide education or insights on a topic they are likely interested in—specifically, about addressing the problems or opportunities they face as part of their day-to-day jobs. Providing this information through a marketing campaign or a seller-initiated email or social media exchange gives prospects some context of what you do and the value you can provide. It also establishes a level of credibility that you understand their world and are much more than someone hawking their wares. Here you should keep any product- or company-related information to the bare minimum—just enough to provide a general idea of what you offer. Whether cold or warm, a seller needs to make a live outreach at some point to complete the prospecting task. To do it well, you need to focus on three things—your message, delivery, and cadence.

MESSAGE

As I said earlier, any live outreach's objective is to raise just enough interest for someone to agree to engage further. Basically, you're looking for a prospect to say, "Sure, I'm up for a dance but with no guarantees on how long." Other than people within weeks of retirement or who perhaps work for certain government agencies, most prospects have jobs that keep them very busy. As such, very few will be all that excited about investing phone, email, or face-to-face time with a stranger without an obvious return on that investment. So, if you're going to have much success, your prospecting message needs to be short, to the point, and compelling. Another analogy I like to use is that your prospecting message needs to be like a roadside billboard. Think about driving down the highway, and you come across a billboard advertising some product or service. Very likely, you will only see it for five to ten seconds. In that time, the ad needs to convey four things—who they are, what they want, why you should care, and what they want you to do. Not only will you see it for a short amount of time, but you're likely busy focusing on other, more important things, like keeping your car on the road. Conveying a billboard message using pictures and graphics in a short amount of time is a whole lot easier than doing it through an email, voicemail, or live conversation, but that's fundamentally what you have to do. And to be effective, the most critical part of any prospecting message is the "Why should they care?" or WIIFT.

While writing this book, I received the following cold prospecting email (modified from the original for the sake of anonymity) that is an example of what not to do:

Hi Greg,

My name is J. Blogs, and I am one of the best in my industry.

More specifically, I am a top, award-winning consultant specializing in the XYZ industry and have helped thousands of companies meet their goals. I don't tell you this to brag, but I am proud of the success I've helped these firms achieve using my unique expertise over the past fifteen years. The services I offer cover a wide range of areas that go well beyond the ones that immediately come to mind, so I'm able to introduce you to many that you might otherwise overlook. I was looking at your background and thought you might be a good fit for what I do.

Now, where's the "Why should I care?" in that? The email was a total of six long, dense paragraphs, all spent describing their services and how great they were. Delete! While I know that this particular email was over the top with bravado, my point is that many prospecting messages are way too much about the seller and way too little about their prospect.

Remember that without the context of a problem or opportunity that someone is interested in addressing, any discussion about an offering makes no sense—unless you happen to be Clerking.

In prospecting, you provide that context through a WIIFT statement. And because the WIIFT is the key to success, it must be stated clearly and as early as possible in your message. But given that you often don't know what problems or opportunities your prospect might be interested in, your strategy is to **Suggest** one or two based on your knowledge of their business. Then **Ask**, just like you would in a typical selling situation, if these are of interest.

Here's an example of a simple, straightforward voicemail message that covers the four key areas listed above in a concise, clear manner:

Hi A. Prospect,

My name is Greg Nutter, and I'm a management consultant specializing in helping companies solve revenue growth challenges (*Who I am*).

The reason I'm calling is that I've been working with sales leaders in your industry that are struggling to get consistent performance across their teams. Relying only on the star performers makes it very difficult to achieve the company's revenue goals (*What do I want* and *Why they should care*).

If this is a concern for you, it would be great to schedule a short call to share what other firms are doing to address this. You can email me at Greg.Nutter@P3Selling.com or give me a call at 123-456-7890 with a couple of dates and times that work best for you (*What do I want them to do*).

I'll also send you an email with my contact information to make it easier to respond. I look forward to speaking with you.

To be most effective, this message should be based on some research that the company was having challenges growing its revenues. Also, if the prospect had engaged with any previous "warm-up" activities, I would want to leverage that as well. For example, I might change the second paragraph to something like this:

> The reason I'm calling is that I noticed you downloaded our recent white paper (or attended our recent webinar, or...) on solving inconsistent performance issues, so I'm guessing this is an area of high interest for you.

The key is to get to the "What do I want, and why you should care" part as quickly as possible—remember the billboard analogy. You have about ten seconds to get there, and your total voicemail message should always be less than thirty seconds.

Here's a summary of best practices when it comes to developing your prospecting message:

- Explain who you are and what you do only for context, and avoid telling people how great you are. It takes up valuable time, and no one really cares at this point.

- Make sure you suggest a problem or opportunity that is highly likely to be one your prospect is facing. Again, here's where either research or looking at past actions is essential. In my example, if I knew the company had growth challenges, the prospect would probably find my suggested Problem highly relatable.

- When describing the Problem, clearly explain how it could

affect them—specifically why they should find it important. Often, we stop at the Problem because its Importance is obvious to us. However, the trigger that causes people to respond is its Importance, not the Problem itself, so you need to state it explicitly.

- Don't offer or describe a solution to the Problem. In fact, I wouldn't even take the time to say that you have one, although your prospect will assume you do. The moment your email sounds like a product pitch, people turn off— unless you happen to hit them on a day when they are actually thinking of buying whatever it is you're pitching. The odds tend not to be in your favor, however. So instead, state that what you are offering are insights on what others are doing.

- Make it clear to the prospect both what you want them to do and what you'll do next. Stating that you will take action conveys that you are serious about reaching them and lets them know what to expect. Lastly, an email follow-up is essential because it's often hard to understand someone's name and contact details when spoken over the phone. If they know you'll be emailing them, they won't get frustrated playing your message a dozen times to capture all the details.

Your follow-up email message will be very similar to the voice-mail, with perhaps slightly more detail around the Problem and its Importance but not around your product or company. It should include your complete contact information, links to your company's website, and perhaps some simple graphics that help explain why you are worthy of a callback. Avoid making the message longer than you can read on a screen without scrolling—generally about three or four short paragraphs. People's eyes roll over when they're busy and find themselves staring at a long, multi-page email.

DELIVERY

My preference is always to start prospecting with a phone call. Often, you'll leave a voicemail, and then follow it with an email. I find this order works best because the sound of your voice tends to humanize an otherwise sterile email message. The two also complement and reinforce each other. When leaving a voicemail, be sure to speak clearly with an unrushed, conversational tone and slowly enough that the prospect can understand you. Many of us often say our names and contact information way too quickly, making them very hard to understand. Practice your script a couple of times before delivering it so you feel comfortable with the flow.

You'll also need to prepare for the rare occasions when, instead of getting someone's voicemail system, you actually get them live. I know this from personal experience when I wasn't prepared and started stumbling over my script. Needless to say, I rapidly went down in flames. While a live message should essentially be the same as your voicemail, the main difference is regular engagement. You'll also need to be super sensitive to the fact that you likely caught your prospect in the middle of doing something important. Rarely will you get someone gazing out the window, waiting for your call.

You engage your prospect by asking simple questions. Many prospectors feel that once they have a person on the phone, they need to rush through their message before getting cut off.

The sooner they get there, they reason, the more likely someone will want to hear more. However, in my experience, speeding through your message is more apt to lead to either a "Thanks but no thanks" or an abrupt hang-up. So here's how I would alter the example above if I happened to reach someone live:

Hi A. Prospect,

My name is Greg Nutter, and I'm a management consultant specializing in helping companies solve revenue growth challenges. **Do you have a moment?**

- *If the answer is NO, tell them that you understand, and ask if another time would work better—perhaps tomorrow or later this week?*

- *If the answer is YES or SURE, continue with your message.*

The reason I'm calling is that I've been working with sales leaders in your industry that are struggling to get consistent performance across their teams. Relying only on the star performers makes it very difficult to achieve the company's revenue goals. **Would this be an area of concern for you?**

- *If NO, validate and suggest another problem. Perhaps I could say something like, "Well, good for you—you're one of the few sales leaders I've come across who have this area under control. Are there other areas, such as forecasting accuracy or big-deal win-rates, that have been worrying you?"*

- *If there's still no interest after suggesting a couple of other problems or opportunities, I could always try the "Hail Mary" question—perhaps asking something like, "Are there any other aspects of your team's sales performance where you would like to see changes?" If still no bite, I would congratulate them on doing a great job and ask if I could check back in six months or a year to see if anything has changed. Then, before hanging up, I would ask if they are interested in a brief overview of what I do and how I'm different from my competitors.*

- *If I get a YES to one of the concerns, continue with the message.*

It would be great to share what other firms are doing to address these issues. **Would now be a good time, or would it be better to schedule another time that works better?**

- *If I got an agreement to discuss a particular Problem further, success—I am now dancing. Lock in a time, and proceed with the first stage of the buying-decision Process.*

Engaging the prospect regularly and offering them control over what happens next demonstrates respect for their time and that you care about what they have to say.

CADENCE

According to research by TeleNet and the Ovation Sales Group, it now takes an average of eight attempts to reach a prospect. Meanwhile, SiriusDecisions reports that the average salesperson only makes two attempts before giving up. No wonder sellers believe that prospecting is a waste of time. The trick is to be persistent without being a pest. Here's what I have found to work well:

1. Start with a phone call where you will likely leave a voice message and immediately follow it up with an email.

2. Wait five to ten days, and repeat the process. I find a week works well but never longer than two weeks. Make another call with the same message, but start by referencing your previous call. You might say something like:

   Hi John/Jill, this is Greg Nutter again. I'm not sure if you received my message from last week or didn't have a chance to reply, so I thought I would reach out again. As I mentioned earlier, I'm a management consultant specializing in helping companies solve revenue growth challenges. The reason I'm calling is…

3. After your voicemail, send out a follow-up email that is also slightly modified to reference your previous call.

4. Repeat this voicemail–email process four to six times. I prefer four times to give you your eight touchpoints, but several companies have told me they get better results by extending the cycle to six. Use your judgment here. If you start getting feedback that you're becoming a pest, ratchet it back a bit.

5. During the last outreach, change both your voice message and email to let the prospect know, in a very respectful way, that this is your final attempt. The key is to validate that it's okay that they didn't respond. For example, your voice message could go something like this:

   Hi John/Jill, this is Greg Nutter again. I'm not sure if you received my messages over the last few weeks, but since I've not heard from you, I'm guessing that either achieving consistent sales performance isn't an issue for you or you are dealing with more pressing challenges. As such, I won't leave you any further messages. However, should things change and you wish to learn more about how others are addressing this, please reach out when the time is right.

Many reps have told me that their prospect responds not long after sending the final email. But, even if they don't, your prospect is more likely to appreciate your respectful approach and save your contact information for future reference.

Even if your final outreach yields no response, you may decide not to totally give up on this prospect. Depending on the size of your territory and the number of potential prospects you have, you could put a reminder in your Customer Relationship Management (CRM) system to follow up with this person in six months to a year. Capturing the date you called them and the Problems you suggested would allow you to start a new prospecting cycle by briefly referencing your past call and suggesting a different potential Problem.

One final comment regarding prospecting. You're probably asking yourself, "If I follow the process as detailed, will I get a response from everyone?" No, you won't. But you will get more responses than others who are reaching out once or twice with a product-oriented pitch. Also, if you stay in the same industry for some time, you will often come across the same prospects down the road. And when you do, they'll remember you as a professional seller who talked about Problems instead of products in a very respectful manner. Prospecting professionally will pay off.

CALL MANAGEMENT

Pretty well all B2B selling happens during a live sales interaction, whether it is over the phone, face to face, or on an online web meeting. Sure, a white paper, webinar, or customer-success story might prime the pump, but it's during those live conversations where the heavy lifting happens. Here, sellers ask questions that increase awareness of the need to solve Problems and suggest ways to optimize the buying-decision Process.

A key challenge for sellers is that live interactions with prospects can be a very scarce commodity. Research by Gartner found that during the buying-decision Process, the average company spends only 17 percent of their time meeting with potential suppliers. And when evaluating multiple suppliers, the amount of time spent with any one sales rep may be only 5 percent or 6 percent. That means if your prospect spends a total of forty hours working through their decision process, you might only get two hours of selling time—not much indeed. Because of this reality, it's imperative to make these calls as successful as possible. Success means moving the buying-decision Process forward in your favor, and to do this consistently requires planning.

"Planning is an unnatural process; it is much more fun to do something. And the nicest thing about not planning is that failure comes as a complete surprise rather than being preceded by a period of worry and depression."
—JOHN HARVEY-JONES, INDUSTRIALIST

Many sales calls end up the same way: unplanned and failing to move the sale forward by very much, although it's always a mystery to me why it would come as a surprise.

That's where call management comes in. It's the process of planning and conducting a call in such a manner that it maximizes your chances of success. I find it works best if you develop your call plan in two steps: first, a high-level plan, followed by a second one that is more detailed and describes the call flow.

HIGH-LEVEL CALL PLAN

There are four areas to think through as part of your high-level plan.

1. Call Objectives

Start by asking yourself "What am I trying to achieve in this call?" based on the expected attendees. For example, is it to understand and influence the prospect's perception of specific Problems, understand their decision criteria, or position your offering versus alternatives? Whatever your objectives, they should align with the prospect's decision stage.

Try not to plan too many objectives. You will likely have a limited amount of time, so it's better to get one or two accomplished than have a bunch that you only get halfway through.

When defining call objectives, an important but sometimes missed part is the WIIFT—what does your prospect get out of this interaction? If you can't clearly describe a compelling WIIFT, then you could have a challenge getting them to agree to a call in the first place. And if you provide one but don't deliver on it during the call, you risk not getting invited back.

2. Desired Outcomes

What end result do you expect or hope for this call? More specifically, what do you want your prospect to do afterward? For example, it could be to introduce you to a key person or provide you with more-detailed financial information. Whatever it is, it should be some action that moves the buying-decision Process forward.

You should also plan for more than one possible outcome. Perhaps a best-case if things go well and a backup if they don't. It's also essential to focus on achieving outcomes regarding what the prospect will do next. Too often, sales reps walk away from a call with all the action items—they agree to send some literature, develop a proposal, follow up in two weeks, or some other activity. The primary measure of a successful call is whether or not you got THEM to agree to do something that moved the sale forward, not you. If you're doing all the work, you are still in the prospecting stage and not working a live opportunity—**you are dancing with yourself!** Be sure that what you're asking them to do is reasonable based on where they are in their decision Process.

3. Areas to Explore

What do you need to understand and influence around how things are and how things should be from both their and your perspectives? At this point, don't worry about writing down specific questions. Just list areas that, based on your call objectives, you need to explore with your prospect. Think in terms of Problems, People, and Processes. Also, consider how you might respond to pushback or objections related to either requesting information or making suggestions.

4. Proposals to Consider

What might you propose to respond to needs uncovered during the "Areas to Explore" step? It could be an overview of your solution and some success stories that link directly to the prospect's Problems. Maybe some suggested actions to engage high-influence people, formalize the buying Process, or uncover and address critical decision criteria. Your proposals should lead the prospect to agree to take specific actions related to the desired outcomes you listed above. Whatever you decide, it should be something that moves the buying-decision Process forward.

DETAILED CALL PLAN

Once you've thought through your high-level plan, you are now in a position to document a plan with more detail. The call flow should align with how individuals make decisions, which we discussed in Chapter 4. This means you will first explore, then share and consider related information, evaluate options on what needs to be done, and finally agree on the next steps. The following five parts of a sales call detail this flow—always the same and always in the same order:

1. Small Talk

The intent here is to break the ice and remove some of the stress associated with the upcoming conversation. Some people are naturals at doing this. If you are not, make a couple of notes on what you might want to share to put people at ease and add a human side to the relationship. While the weather and latest sports scores are good standbys, something more topical about the company you're visiting can help establish your business credentials.

The amount of time spent on small talk can vary depending on the local culture and amount of time allocated for your call. North Americans typically expect only a few minutes, while some Asian, Middle Eastern, and African cultures expect more—sometimes even the majority of the call. Germanic and Scandinavian cultures often prefer to get right down to business. Remember that these are generalities, so always try to read your prospect for cues when it's time to move on.

Finally, if new people are in the meeting, this is an excellent time to introduce them and explain their role in the buying-decision Process.

2. Introduction

This step is a key part of a successful call and one that many reps do poorly. If your prospect knows where you are going, why, and how you plan to get there, they will almost always agree to follow along. If they don't know where you are going or why, you run the risk of getting pushback, or worse—having the prospect hijack your call in a direction that is not to your advantage.

Your introduction will consist of stating and gaining agreement on three things:

1. **Objective.** State the purpose or objective of the call and why it is valuable for them. You should also share what you hope the outcomes will be if all goes well.

2. **Agenda.** Outline what topics you want to cover and in what order. Confirm the amount of time your prospect has allocated for this call so you can plan accordingly. Be sure to

ask if there is anything else your prospect would like discussed. If they suggest something that isn't critical but could sidetrack the meeting, ask if covering it at the end or in a subsequent call would be acceptable.

3. **Agreement.** Finally, ask if they are okay with the call objective and agenda you've shared.

3. Explore

This step is almost always the most crucial part of a call because it's where you actually engage in selling. Typically, you will spend most of your call time here, and doing it well will require the most pre-call planning. Often, you'll start by confirming what you know or have heard from other sources before asking about new information. Then, explore the areas from your high-level plan using the Ask↔Suggest:Recap Sales Play.

Because it's hard for most of us to ask good questions on the fly, you should write out the most important ones in advance. Plan the conversation flow to explore at a big-picture level first and gradually move to the details. You should also note what you plan to suggest and the rationale you will use as justification. Finally, document your reasoning to counter any objections you might come across.

While you can Recap at the end of each discussion area, you always want one final Recap that summarizes all that was covered.

4. Propose

This step is about collaboratively responding to the gaps you just explored between the current state and the desired state. Here, you focus on answering the question "What could we do to solve this?" You will often suggest one or more approaches, but it's always good to ask what your buyer would recommend first. Depending on what you uncovered in the Explore step, there are many things you might want to propose. Here are two examples:

- "Well, Jim/Jill—based on the reliability issues you're having with your service provider and how important it is to get it resolved, now might be a good time to share some of our company's capabilities. Would this work for you, or is there something we should do first?"

- "Well, Jim/Jill—based on what you've told me about how your company makes purchasing decisions, I think we need to engage your vice president to get the ball rolling. I have a few ideas on how we could do this, but I'll bet you've been in this situation before. What would you suggest we do?"

Wherever you are in the decision Process, you should always try to get your prospect to consider multiple options because having thought through more than one gives them the confidence necessary to make their final decision. And ideally, you want them to go through this brainstorming process with your guidance rather than with your competitor's. So if you were talking about your solution, brainstorm various options on how they might deploy it. Or, if the conversation is around engaging the vice president, you might share a couple of options that have worked well for you in the past—perhaps a high-level strategy presentation, a cross-functional workshop, or just a call from your company's senior management.

Once you have a few options on the table, turn your attention to positioning them—what are the pros and cons of each. Ask and suggest until you and your prospect have agreed on the best way forward. I like to ask my prospect, "What do you think the best next step should be?" as sometimes they'll propose a more significant step than I was thinking. If they come back with something smaller, then it's time to suggest, explain the rationale, and ask for their agreement.

5. Summary and Action Plan

This step is small but significant because it ensures that everyone's on the same page before leaving the meeting. Here, you summarize the key outcomes of the call: what you agreed to work on from the Explore step, what options you considered from the Propose step, and lastly, what you decided were the best next steps. These next steps become your action plan, clearly stated in terms of "What specifically will be done," "By whom," and "By when."

You'll also need to agree on when a follow-up should occur to check on the action plan's status. As mentioned earlier, you should do your best to ensure that you aren't the only one agreeing to do things. Sure, there might be one or two initial calls where you may have to do all the work. But after that, if your prospect is not taking on any meaningful activities to move the sale forward, you need to ask yourself if you should be spending your valuable time elsewhere.

Finally, wrap up the call by thanking them for their time, and finish with any additional small talk.

I highly recommend sending a short email following your call to document your Summary and agreed Action Plan. You probably took good notes, but not all prospects do, so be sure to put it in writing. Not only does this demonstrate your professionalism, but it will make things much easier when you do your next follow-up.

Almost every sales interaction will follow this exact same flow, although the content will change depending on the meeting participants and your call objectives. So when planning your call, write out the five steps above and add your notes and critical questions. And be sure to refer to your notes during the meeting to keep you on track.

OPPORTUNITY MANAGEMENT

At the end of the day, selling is all about winning deals. As good as we are with our prospecting and call management, we won't keep our jobs for long without putting some numbers on the scoreboard. That's why good opportunity management is a crucial part of your ongoing success. Opportunity management is about three things:

1. Defining where you are in a specific opportunity's buying-decision Process.

2. Establishing your key selling objectives and activities based on that position.

3. Developing, executing, and revising action plans that move the deal forward.

A typical mistake some sellers make is to think that what they are doing defines an opportunity's decision stage. For example, if they are presenting a proposal, they must be in the Evaluate Alternatives stage. Or, if they just made their first prospecting call, the customer is in the Prospect stage. By making these mistakes, you can engage in certain activities at the wrong time, lowering your chances of winning. Instead, we must look at what the prospect is thinking and doing, as that alone defines where you are in the Process. Sound opportunity management depends on this concept.

So, your first step is to define where you are in the buying Process based on the prospect's perceptions and actions. Table 1, below, is a tool to help you do this. Note that "prospect" refers to all the people involved in the buying decision, not just your key contacts.

TABLE 1: DEFINING THE BUYING-DECISION STAGE

IF YOUR PROSPECT'S PERSPECTIVES OR ACTIONS ARE THESE...	THEN YOU ARE IN THIS BUYING-DECISION STAGE

• Low or no recognition of
  ◦ A Problem (problem or opportunity), OR
  ◦ The Importance of addressing a Problem, OR
  ◦ The availability or practicality of a solution to address a Problem
• Unsure if what a seller is proposing is applicable, of value, reasonable, or credible for their situation
• Uncertain whether they have enough interest to invest more time
• No buying-decision Process in place
	PROSPECT

• Awareness of one or more Problems that may require addressing
• Expresses interest in learning more about
  ◦ The Importance (Impact and Urgency) of addressing the identified Problems
  ◦ The availability or practicality of solutions to address the identified Problems
• Willing to share information about their situation and Problems and the Importance of addressing them
• Low/no commitment to take further action
• No buying-decision Process in place
	NEED RECOGNITION

IF YOUR PROSPECT'S PERSPECTIVES OR ACTIONS ARE THESE...	THEN YOU ARE IN THIS BUYING-DECISION STAGE

• Decides that one or more Problems are important enough to consider addressing
• Takes action to
  ◦ Establish a buying-decision Process
  ◦ Engage others to gain support for a buying Process
• Invests time to learn more about
  ◦ Options available to address the Problems
  ◦ How other companies have addressed the Problems
  ◦ Expected costs, risks, investments, and benefits related to addressing the Problems
• Conducts internal research on
  ◦ Decision constraints—e.g., existing contractual obligations, budget availability, other compliance requirements
  ◦ Decision participants' support (prioritization and timing) for addressing the Problems
• Conducts external research through
  ◦ Social media
  ◦ Peers and industry groups
  ◦ Supplier websites
  ◦ Analysts or industry reports
• Analyzes and gains consensus on risk/reward of taking or not taking action
	INFORMATION SEARCH

• Fully defines Problems and solution scope
• Establishes buying-decision criteria
  ◦ Desired business benefits and outcomes
  ◦ Financials: budget, ROI, resources, etc.
  ◦ Supplier-selection criteria
  ◦ Compliance requirements
• Formalizes buying-decision Process
  ◦ Participants
  ◦ Steps
• Creates/distributes RFP and compiles supplier submissions
• Resolves gaps in information
• Evaluates alternative approaches and suppliers against the decision criteria
	EVALUATE ALTERNATIVES

IF YOUR PROSPECT'S PERSPECTIVES OR ACTIONS ARE THESE…	→	THEN YOU ARE IN THIS BUYING- DECISION STAGE

• Selects supplier or makes a no-go decision
• Resolves outstanding concerns
• Resolves mixed emotions
  ◦ Excitement over taking action to address
    Problems
    versus
  ◦ Concern over the risk of making a mistake
• Finalizes supplier negotiations:
  pricing, contract terms, etc.
• Finalizes implementation plan
• Assigns or allocates resources
• Commits funds
		PURCHASE DECISION

Table 1 applies to both the individual and the corporate buying-decision Processes, and so it's not uncommon to find people in different stages. For example, some people in the Consensus Stream might be much further along than those in the Compliance Stream, while others, whom you've not had much contact with, may be barely out of the Prospect stage. However, the actions and perspectives of people in the Compliance Stream tend to define the corporate Process stage. Also, bear in mind that sometimes you will prospect your way into a decision Process that's well underway—like when, after a prospecting call, a surprise RFP shows up in your inbox. In these cases, you will need to do your best to pull your prospect back a stage or two so that you can engage in some crucial selling. If you can't, you might have to resign yourself to Clerking and finger-crossing.

Once you've decided which stage your prospect is in, you then establish your key selling objectives and activities based on that stage. This two-step process helps you avoid common errors that can negatively impact your chances of winning the deal. Table 2, below, is a guide to help do this.

TABLE 2: ESTABLISHING SELLING OBJECTIVES AND KEY ACTIVITIES

IF YOUR PROSPECT IS IN THIS BUYING-DECISION STAGE →	THEN YOUR SELLING OBJECTIVES AND KEY ACTIVITIES ARE...

PROSPECT	Selling Objective:
	
	• Create sufficient interest so the prospect agrees to explore their potential Problems further
	
	Key Activities:
	
	• Pre-call research, qualification, and message development
	  ◦ Assess prospect fit to target customer profiles
	  ◦ Estimate opportunity
	  ◦ Conduct company research
	  ◦ Establish ideal entry contact
	  ◦ Select possible Problems to suggest
	  ◦ Develop prospecting script (live, voicemail, and email)
	• Initiate prospect warm-up activities, if possible
	• Initiate prospecting message cycle—call, voicemail, email, and repeat
	• Gain agreement with prospects on date/time to explore Problems further
	
	Common Errors:
	
	• Pitching your product, price, solution, or company
	• Failing to do sufficient research before engaging
	• Delivering a long or complex message
	• Failing to state the Impact of suggested Problems
	• Failing to confirm interest and gain agreement on exploring Problems further

IF YOUR PROSPECT IS IN THIS BUYING-DECISION STAGE →	THEN YOUR SELLING OBJECTIVES AND KEY ACTIVITIES ARE...
NEED RECOGNITION	Selling Objective:

Selling Objective:

- Develop sufficient awareness around specific Problems and their Importance so that the prospect agrees to take action toward addressing them

Key Activities:

- Ask↔Suggest:Recap to
  - Understand the prospect's current situation
  - Understand and influence the prospect's perspective of all potential Problems
  - Understand and influence the prospect's awareness of the Impact and Urgency of addressing the Problems from both a personal and business perspective
  - Understand and influence the prospect's awareness of how the Problems affect other people
- Qualify the prospect's ability (resources, timing, role, authority, and other constraints) to address the identified Problems
- Establish the seller's credibility to help address the Problems
- Understand, influence, and gain agreement on specific actions that the seller and prospect will take to move a buying-decision Process forward

Common Errors:

- Pitching detailed product, price, solution, or company information
- Telling instead of asking or suggesting
- Advancing to the next stage after identifying only inconsequential Problems or Problems that competitors are better suited to address
- Failing to create sufficient awareness around the Importance of addressing the Problems
- Failing to understand who else is affected by the identified Problems
- Failing to qualify the opportunity fully
- Taking ownership for all actions

IF YOUR PROSPECT IS IN THIS BUYING-DECISION STAGE →	THEN YOUR SELLING OBJECTIVES AND KEY ACTIVITIES ARE...

INFORMATION SEARCH	Selling Objective:
	
	• Guide and support the prospect in gathering sufficient information to confidently evaluate solution alternatives
	
	Key Activities:
	
	• Understand and influence Problem perspectives of other affected decision participants
	• Understand and influence decision participants' preconceived solution perspectives
	• Anticipate, understand, and influence each decision participant's information requirements for them to confidently evaluate solution alternatives
	• Anticipate, understand, and influence potential internal decision constraints
	• Brainstorm solution options with key decision participants
	• Provide Problem-relevant solution information
	  ◦ Success stories, business cases, and references
	  ◦ Configuration, pricing, and deployment options
	• Suggest credible external information sources
	• Anticipate, understand, and influence the buying-decision Process
	• Suggest ways to simplify and expedite the buying-decision Process
	
	Common Errors:
	
	• Spending insufficient time guiding and supporting the prospect in this stage
	• Failing to anticipate and proactively engage all those involved in the buying decision
	• Failing to understand and influence the perspectives of all those involved in the buying decision
	• Failing to build confidence that sufficient information has been sourced and reviewed
	• Overwhelming prospects by providing too much information or information that is not specific to addressing the identified Problems
	• Providing too many solution options that complicate the decision Process
	• Taking ownership for all actions

IF YOUR PROSPECT IS IN THIS BUYING-DECISION STAGE $\rightarrow$	THEN YOUR SELLING OBJECTIVES AND KEY ACTIVITIES ARE...

EVALUATE ALTERNATIVES	Selling Objective:
	
	• Guide and support the prospect in formalizing an efficient and effective solution-evaluation Process
	
	Key Activities:
	
	• Understand and influence the Problem and solution scope
	• Understand and influence the prospect's perspectives of alternative solutions
	• Understand and influence buying-decision criteria
	  ◦ Desired business benefits and outcomes
	  ◦ Financial requirements: budget, ROI, resources, etc.
	  ◦ Supplier-acceptance criteria
	  ◦ Solution and supplier-ranking criteria
	  ◦ Compliance requirements
	• Provide boilerplate RFP template (if required)
	• Collaboratively develop a solution that best meets the decision criteria
	• Present solution with messaging aligned to decision-influencer perspectives on addressing the Problems
	• Provide clear positioning of the solution versus the alternatives
	
	Common Errors:
	
	• Telling versus asking and suggesting
	• Failing to influence the buying-decision Process and criteria proactively
	• Failing to specifically link solution features to buying-decision criteria
	• Developing the final solution without key decision-participant involvement
	• Failing to provide clear differentiation between the proposed solution and the alternatives
	• Taking ownership for all actions

IF YOUR PROSPECT IS IN THIS BUYING-DECISION STAGE →	THEN YOUR SELLING OBJECTIVES AND KEY ACTIVITIES ARE...

PURCHASE DECISION	Selling Objective:
	
	• Guide and support the prospect in making a confident final-purchase decision
	
	Key Activities:
	
	• Collaboratively develop and manage a final-step project plan
	  ◦ What activities does the prospect's company need to do to complete the purchase?
	  ◦ What activities does the seller's company need to do to complete the sale?
	  ◦ Who will do what, and by when?
	• Anticipate and collaboratively resolve last-minute obstacles and concerns
	• Conduct final negotiations
	• Close for commitment to action
	
	Common Errors:
	
	• Failing to expedite the completion of all final steps
	• Closing too hard when key decision-makers are hesitant due to lack of decision confidence
	• Ignoring concerns and hoping they will go away on their own

P3 SELLING DEAL REVIEW

The third important part of opportunity management is a P3 Selling Deal Review. This is where you assess your situation relative to the P3 Selling concepts and then develop the best action plan to move a buying decision forward. It involves stopping for a moment to reflect where you are and thoughtfully decide what you should do next—kind of like standing back from the trees so you can see the forest. Choosing whether or how often to conduct a Review depends on the deal's importance. If it's one that you must win, then you should conduct a review at least monthly, or whenever you're unsure what to do next. Some top sellers conduct a Review of critical deals every week.

The starting point for a Deal Review is establishing what Problems you are trying to solve. You can't develop an effective selling strategy until you define these—you can only Clerk products. Unfortunately, some sales strategy methodologies start by asking the question "What products am I trying to sell?" I think this is a mistake for two reasons. First, it's limiting. It's kind of like the old adage, "If all you have is a hammer, everything looks like a nail." If you start with the perspective of "What am I trying to sell," then every action you take tends to look like a product pitch. Instead, if you start with a problem or opportunity perspective, you have many more options on how to address them. Second, focusing on problems and opportunities puts you on the same side of the table as your prospect. Instead of arm wrestling over a product decision, you are part of the team collaborating on a Problem-solving decision.

A P3 Selling Deal Review involves asking yourself several questions in five critical areas. This process allows you to understand your current state, assess your risks, and develop an action plan for the best things to do next. In answering these questions, it's okay to say "I don't know" or "I'm not sure." This is a crucial part of pinpointing areas of uncertainty and, hence, risk. Likewise, it's not okay to guess or assume—instead, be brutally honest about what you are sure of and what you're not. Follow the steps below and use your answers to develop an action plan:

P3 Selling Deal Review Process

1. Problems (problems or opportunities):
   A. What Problems has your prospect explicitly stated interest in addressing?
   B. Which Problems can you address more effectively than alternatives?
   C. What are your prospect's perspectives regarding the Impact and Urgency of addressing these? Personally and corporately? Have you quantified the Impact of not addressing the Problems?
   D. From your prospect's perspective, is the Importance of addressing these Problems large enough to warrant the time, investment, and potential risk involved in making a purchase decision?
   E. What are your prospect's perceptions regarding alternatives to addressing the Problems?

2. People:
   A. Who are all the people expected to be involved in the company's buying-decision Process?
      I. Problem People
      II. Process People
   B. How confident are you that you know all the people involved?
   C. What is the level of Decision Influence for each of these people?
   D. For Problem People with a high level of Decision Influence, what are their perspectives regarding each Problem's Impact and Urgency?
   E. For Process People with a high level of Decision Influence:
      I. In which buying-Process steps will they be involved?

      ii. What criteria are they likely to focus on?

      iii.What are their perspectives regarding the "correct" decision criteria?

3. Processes:
   A. Who initiated the buying-decision Process, when, and why?
   B. In which buying-decision stages are people with a high level of Decision Influence (refer to TABLE 1: Defining the Buying-Decision Stage)?
   C. What does the company's stated buying-decision Process look like (people, steps, timeline, etc.)?
   D. Which elements of the decision Process (steps, criteria, policies, people, information sources, etc.):
      i. Highlight our solution strengths?
      ii. Highlight our competitors' or other alternatives' strengths?

4. Analysis:
   A. Where do we lack or are unsure of critical Problem, People, or Process information?
      i. What have people not specifically said or done to confirm our understanding?
      ii. How confident are we in the information our primary contacts have provided?
   B. What are our risks?
   C. Problems:
      i. Is there a low awareness of Problems that we can solve?
      ii. Is there a low awareness of the Importance in addressing the identified Problems?
      iii.Is the quantified Impact of not addressing the Prob-

lems large enough to warrant the effort and risk involved in making a buying decision?

IV. Are there alternatives to our solution that can address the identified Problems equally well or better?

D. People:

I. Are there only a small number of people involved in the buying decision that are aware of the identified Problems?

II. Are there only a small number of people involved in the buying decision that perceive addressing the Problems as important?

III. Have all people involved in the buying decision been identified?

IV. Are there people with high Decision Influence with a preference for an alternative way of addressing the Problems (not with us)?

V. Are there people with high Decision Influence whom we've not understood and influenced their perspectives?

E. Process:

I. Are there people with high Decision Influence at different stages in the buying-decision Process?

II. Have people progressed to late stages in the buying-decision Process where we have not had an opportunity to understand and influence their perspectives on Problems, People, or Processes?

III. Are there people highly motivated to address the identified Problems that are not part of the buying-decision Process?

IV. Have we provided information that focuses on the identified Problems and aligns with each individual's decision stage?

     v. Are there any compliance constraints that would make a buying decision difficult at this time (contractual, budget, etc.)?

5. Actions:
    A. What are all the things we could do next to:
       i. Address our information gaps (unknown or unsure)
       ii. Reduce our current risks
       iii. Advance people to the next decision stage (refer to TABLE 2: Establishing Selling Objectives and Key Activities)?
    B. Consolidate the list above where possible and select the highest priority and impactful actions.
    C. For each action, consider what credible resources you could leverage to increase your odds of success. For example, what people (theirs, yours, external), tools, documents, demos, etc., would help you gain access to a critical decision participant, create greater awareness, or resolve a potential constraint?
    D. Decide on who will do what and by when

Since the P3 Selling Deal Review combines analysis and brainstorming, it often works better with a small group of sales professionals. In a group setting, start by briefly sharing all that has occurred to date. Follow-up group Reviews should begin by sharing the actions completed since the previous Review and their outcomes.

PIPELINE MANAGEMENT

The last topic in our P3 Selling Playbook is pipeline management.

Some people confuse pipeline management and opportunity management by using the terms interchangeably. They are quite different. As discussed above, opportunity management is about *developing and executing the best action plans to move a specific opportunity forward.* Doing so maximizes your chances of winning each deal. Pipeline management is about *prioritizing your overall activities to ensure a steady, predictable stream of sales revenue.* The graphic below illustrates this difference:

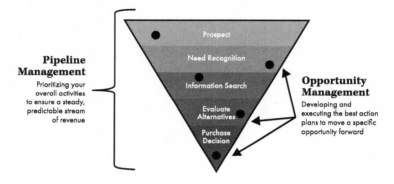

Pipeline management tells you three things: the highest priority activities to focus on, in which order, and the sales performance to expect in the near to mid-term. It utilizes a seller's pipeline, which is a snapshot in time of the buying-decision stages of each potential sales opportunity. For pipeline management to work effectively, opportunities need to be updated regularly, typically using a company's CRM system.

At the risk of stating the obvious, many sellers aren't fans of managing their CRM pipelines because they often see little personal value in doing so. The process tends to feel like a time-consuming exercise in data entry with the sole purpose of keeping management updated in case the seller moves on to greener pastures. Not a lot of WIIFT from the seller's perspective.

However, in reality, there is a lot for sellers to gain through effective pipeline management, provided they take a disciplined approach to updating their pipeline and prioritizing their activities based on what it tells them.

THE REAL VALUE OF GOOD PIPELINE MANAGEMENT IS IT TELLS YOU WHERE TO SPEND YOUR TIME IF YOU WANT TO BE SUCCESSFUL.

THE GOLDEN RULE OF PIPELINE MANAGEMENT

First, there is a golden rule if you want to make pipeline management work for you:

AN OPPORTUNITY'S STAGE IS ALWAYS BASED ON WHAT THE PROSPECT IS DOING, NOT THE SELLER.

I know I've mentioned this several times earlier, but here, it's essential. And often, the biggest obstacle to following this rule is the people who set up the company's CRM system in the first place. For example, one popular CRM vendor describes the main stages in an opportunity pipeline as Prospecting, Lead Qualification, Demo or Meeting, Proposal, Negotiation and Commitment, and Opportunity Won. Now tell me—does this mostly describe what the prospect is doing or what the seller is doing? In fact, if you Google "sales pipeline stages," you'll come up with many variations of the above, with most based on what the seller is doing, not the prospect. In my opinion, this is one of the fundamental challenges with effective pipeline management. Sellers should never develop action plans based on what they've done—only on what the prospect is doing.

When the terminology is wrong, a sales rep will often place an opportunity in the CRM's proposal stage just because they've given a quote—even though the prospect hasn't decided whether or not they're going to do anything. When this happens, management thinks a purchase decision is imminent and directs the seller to conduct the next logical action—close the deal. And we all know that is not what they should be doing, given the prospect's state of mind. Some managers push back and tell me that their reps aren't stupid enough to create a proposal before a client is ready to receive it. Maybe, although in my experience, the practice is quite common. Either way, it leads to confusion, which is not what you want when managing your pipeline. My advice—use Table 1 to decide the appropriate stage for each opportunity.

WITHOUT A CONSISTENT APPROACH TO ASSESSING OPPORTUNITIES THAT INCLUDES A COMMON LANGUAGE, METRICS, AND PROCESSES THAT MINIMIZE SUBJECTIVITY, PIPELINE MANAGEMENT IS A WASTE OF TIME.

Okay, so if you know how to designate the correct buying stages for each opportunity, you're in a position to conduct a meaningful Pipeline Review. This five-step process, which is at the core of pipeline management, helps you define and prioritize your most important activities. The process is detailed as follows.

P3 SELLING PIPELINE REVIEW PROCESS
1. Review and Update Each Opportunity's Stage

Opportunities move forward and backward in the buying-decision Process no matter how good a seller you are. So before going any further, you want to be sure you are working with the latest information. I recommend doing a stage review and update for each opportunity at least weekly. A key success factor in this is to be brutally honest on where things are. Being optimistic is undoubtedly a virtue, unless it's your outlook when performing either a Deal or Pipeline Review. We all would like to have our deals advancing nicely, with many in the final stages of closing. But in reality, that rarely happens. The key is to judge every opportunity with cold, cruel honesty—anything else is likely to lead you astray.

A critical part of the Review is determining whether an opportunity is still alive. Having deals in your pipeline that have long since expired is both a distraction and a time-waster. They lull you into thinking you have more revenue opportunities than you have—tricking you into believing you don't need to do much prospecting. They also take up your valuable time when you continue to follow up. So you need to decide if the opportunity still belongs in your pipeline by asking yourself this question—are they still dancing? Dancing means that someone in the company is performing tangible actions to move the buying decision forward. Dancing means more than simply returning your phone calls and emails or letting you take them for lunch.

Start by establishing a timeframe on when to make your assessment. Typically, sellers use sixty or ninety days, but depending on the average length of your sales cycles, the timeframe could be as short as thirty days or as long as six months. Whatever you decide, assess each opportunity by asking yourself if anyone has performed a meaningful action to move the buying Process forward in the past set timeframe. If the answer is no, close out the deal from your pipeline. Now, I know this is a difficult, often-emotional decision, and many sellers resist doing it. But without a candid assessment of where things are, you won't make good decisions on how best to spend your time. Making this call doesn't mean there will never be an opportunity with this account—it just means there isn't one right now. If you think this opportunity is still worthy of pursuing, move it back to the Prospect stage with a zero-dollar value or set a future reminder to reach out again. The critical thing is to get rid of deals from your pipeline that are simply wishful thinking.

2. Develop Actions for All Opportunities All at Once

I've heard it said that at its core, management is all about three things: making lists, doing things on the list, and then making new lists, no matter what it is you're managing. So once you've updated each opportunity's stage, make a list of all the logical next-step actions to move them forward.

Use both Table 2 and outputs from any recent P3 Selling Deal Reviews as your guide. Listing actions for all opportunities before the "doing" part lets you prioritize some over others to ensure the important ones get done first.

3. Calculate Pipeline Needed versus Actuals

Now comes the step that can be either depressing or motivating—calculating the total value of your pipeline and comparing it against what you need to achieve your sales quota.

Start by calculating an estimate of how much you need to have. There are many ways to do this, but the following equation is probably the most straightforward:

$$\underset{\substack{\text{(for a Particular}\\\text{Period in Months)}}}{\substack{\textbf{Sales Quota}\\\textbf{or Target}}} \times \frac{\substack{\textbf{Average Sales}\\\textbf{Cycle Length}\\\text{(in Months)}}}{\substack{\textbf{\# of Months}\\\textbf{in the Period}}} \times \frac{1}{\substack{\textbf{Average}\\\textbf{Opportunity}\\\textbf{Win Rate}}} = \mathbf{?}$$

For example, let's say you have a $1 million sales quota over a twelve-month period, your Average Sales Cycle Length is four months, and your Average Win-Rate is about 33 percent. Here's how much you need in your pipeline:

$$\underset{\text{(over 12 Months)}}{\mathbf{\$1,000,000}} \times \frac{\substack{\textbf{Average}\\\textbf{4-Month}\\\textbf{Sales Cycle}}}{\substack{\textbf{12 Months}\\\textbf{in the Period}}} \times \frac{1}{33\%} = \underset{\text{(Pipeline Needed)}}{\mathbf{\$1,000,000}}$$

Similarly, if all the above numbers were the same except that your Average Sales Cycle Length was six months, you would need to have a pipeline worth $1,500,000. The calculation works best if you pick a sales quota for a period longer than your Average Sales Cycle Length. Sellers who are unsure of their Average Win-Rate will often select a percentage between 33 percent and 25 percent. If you are in a very competitive market, it can be as low as 15 percent to 20 percent, or if your opportunities are very well qualified, it can be as high as 50 percent. Generally, the rule of thumb is to use 33 percent.

Now add up the estimated value of all opportunities in your pipeline and compare that to what you just calculated. Opportunities in the Prospect stage should always have a zero-dollar value because your potential buyers aren't dancing with you yet. In many cases, after performing this calculation, your first reaction will be "holy crap" or some other expletive because you don't have nearly enough opportunities to make your plan. This is when a wave of depression tends to set in. However, once you've regained your composure, it's time to get motivated to address the gap. There are two ways to do it. You can increase the win-rate for your existing deals or increase the size of your pipeline. Each is a reasonable strategy, although the most successful reps do both.

4. Prioritize All Your Activities

Selling is a reasonably complex job. There are many different kinds of activities, each with a different level of payoff as it relates to achieving your goals. So, without putting together an action plan that prioritizes the important activities over others, it's easy to spend too much time on the wrong things—and not enough time on the things that truly move the needle.

As Stephen Covey, author of *The Seven Habits of Highly Effective People*, famously promoted, "What is important is seldom urgent and what is urgent is seldom important." That's why this step is critical to your success. To avoid getting caught up in the "urgent but not important" stuff, prioritize your activities in the following order:

- **First: Complete all critical activities related to opportunities in the Purchase Decision stage.** If you remember, back in Chapter 4, we called this stage the "Danger Zone." That's because unforeseen events can cause your prospect to lose confidence, delaying or terminating their purchase decision. The longer your prospect is in this stage, the greater the risk that your deal goes south. So your first priority is to complete all activities to close these deals as quickly as possible.

- **Second: Prospect for new opportunities to close the "Pipeline Needed versus Actuals" gap.** Many sellers leave prospecting to the very last, which often means not doing enough or not doing any at all. New opportunities usually take the most time to travel through your pipeline, so if you wait until all other deals have closed or stalled, it will be some time before you can drag a new one out of the other end. High-performing sellers consistently prioritize weekly chunks of time to focus on this crucial task.

- **Third: Complete activities that advance early-stage opportunities.** Remember that buyers will spend more time in early stages if the decision appears complex or risky. As a result, it will often take more time and effort to move prospects through the Need Recognition and Information Search stages than later ones. The mistake we often make is to spend too much time on deals in the Evaluate Alternatives stage, which keeps us from working on opportunities that are much more dependent on our selling activities to advance.

- **Fourth: Conduct P3 Selling Deal Reviews on all must-win opportunities, ideally with your sales peers or managers.**

Deal Reviews are critical for developing the optimum action plan to move things forward, which is key to increasing your win-rate. They can also bring attention to a prospect that is no longer dancing, so you can stop wasting further time on them.

- **Fifth: Complete all other sales-related activities,** such as those associated with deals in the Evaluate Alternatives stage, returning non-urgent calls and emails, and other personal-development tasks.

5. Calendarize Your Activities in Blocks

When I was in high school, a science teacher showed us this experiment. On the table were three containers, each filled with different materials. The first had large rocks, the second had mid-sized stones, and the last one contained sand. The goal was to get as much material as possible into one large bucket. His first attempt started with filling the bucket with sand, then adding the stones, and finally, the rocks. As you might expect, it wouldn't all fit. But, when he tried again, he reversed the order—big rocks first, followed by stones, and lastly, the sand. To our surprise, the bucket now held all the material with ease. Many personal performance experts use this analogy to illustrate the importance of putting the "big rocks" in first when scheduling your time. This way, you are more likely to get the essential activities done and let the less-important things either fill in the gaps or not get done at all.

Based on the prioritization exercise above, you now know which buckets are more important than others—so you'll add them to your calendar in precisely that order. If they won't all fit, either move lower-priority activities to a later date or make a conscious decision not to do them.

One important set of big rocks we didn't address earlier are the ones you have to do to keep your job. Stuff like team meetings, manager one-on-ones, company meetings, sales forecasting, scheduled training, and other items that aren't optional. Start by blocking time in your calendar for each of these key company activities. Then block off time for each bucket of activities according to their priority:

1. Purchase Decision stage activities first,

2. Prospecting second,

3. Early-stage activities third,

4. And so on…

For example, perhaps you'll block off Monday from 8:00 a.m. to 10:00 a.m. to work on Purchase Decision stage activities; from 1:00 p.m. to 2:00 p.m., you'll put together a prospecting target list, then plan to make prospecting calls for two hours Tuesday morning. Leave some space between the "big rocks" to do the little things that always pop up, like returning calls, replying to emails, or taking part in unplanned meetings. However you allocate your time, it has to allow you to follow it consistently. During those blocked times, do your best to ignore the urgent but less important things that inevitably crop up—the phone rings, an email shows up in your inbox, a coworker stops by for a chat. You'll also have to make adjustments for unscheduled events on occasion, such as finding a time that works for everyone when organizing a P3 Selling Deal Review. An essential part of managing these adjustments is when you're forced to book something new in place of a previously allocated time block. In such cases, you should immediately reschedule that block in place of some other activity with lower priority.

It's best to calendarize blocks of time for categories of activities instead of for every single action. Otherwise, your calendar will be so detailed that it becomes useless. But, if you have an activity that must get completed by a specific date, such as an RFP response or a customer presentation, you should calendarize a block of time dedicated specifically to getting that done.

What works best for many sellers is to do a weekly Pipeline Review and Activity Calendarization every Friday afternoon so they know exactly which activities to focus on when they arrive on Monday morning.

KEY TAKEAWAYS

Today's sellers rely on more than just their skills and activity levels to be consistently successful. They leverage repeatable, sound sales processes to keep them on track. While there are many sales processes that help manage different aspects of the sales job, we focused on the four most critical ones:

1. **Prospecting,** done well and consistently, is key to most sellers' success. It's a process to create initial interest around problems or opportunities AND qualify a prospect's interest and ability to address them. There are four success factors to maximize the chances of establishing a viable sales opportunity, either for now or in the future: pre-call research and

warm-up, a compelling and concise message, an engaging delivery, and a disciplined cadence.

2. **Call Management** is the process of planning and conducting a sales call to maximize the chances of moving a buying decision forward. Sellers first develop a high-level call plan followed by a more detailed one that describes the call flow. The high-level plan defines the call's objectives, outcomes, areas to explore, and proposals to present. The detailed plan covers five steps that always flow in the same order, no matter what kind of call you're having. Following up each call with an email summary of the discussion and agreed actions is a best practice to keep moving the buying decision forward.

3. **Opportunity Management** is a structured approach to maximize the chances of winning your most important sales opportunities. It involves assessing where you are in the buying-decision Process so you can develop the best action plans to move the deal forward. At the heart of opportunity management is the five-step P3 Selling Deal Review process, in which you ask yourself key questions to develop the best action plan. You should conduct a Deal Review, either individually or as a group, whenever you have a "must-win" opportunity that requires you to be more strategic instead of reactive.

4. **Pipeline Management** is a process that helps sellers prioritize their activities to ensure a steady flow of sales revenue. It tells you which activities to focus on, in what order, and what sales performance you should expect. Effective pipeline management requires a regular Pipeline Review to define, prioritize, and calendarize a seller's most important tasks.

Our next and final chapter is about preparing you for "The Journey Beyond"—how you can make P3 Selling a consistent part of your daily routine so that the success it offers can be yours. But before you begin, use the four important activities below to start applying the P3 Selling Playbook processes in your world.

MAKE IT YOUR OWN

Using the P3 Selling Playbook processes to manage your sales success requires thinking and working a little differently. In particular, you will need to force yourself to periodically step away from the day-to-day action of phone calls, emails, meetings, and proposals to develop more strategic plans. This can be tough at first. So, to get you started, here are a few things you should do right away:

1. Create a prospecting script using the best practices described earlier in this chapter. In my experience, it will often take several tries before you get one that is really good. Be sure to edit it for brevity and minimize any product or company information. Focus your message on suggesting a problem or an opportunity, not a product or solution—pitching a solution while prospecting comes across as Clerking. For example, in my sample prospecting email, the message was about "struggling to get consistent performance," not "struggling to get sales skills and process training." Consistent performance was the problem, while skills and process training would have been my solution.

2. Pick a critical, upcoming client meeting or phone call and develop a call plan. Start by creating a high-level plan and then use it to document your detailed call flow. After the

call, compare what happened versus your plan: what areas were missed, where should the plan have had more detail, what went well, what could you do better next time? Then pick another upcoming call, and repeat the process.

3. Select one of your must-win sales opportunities to conduct a P3 Selling Deal Review, ideally with a small group of your peers. Then follow the process step by step and be sure to be brutally honest with yourself and others about which facts you are sure of and which you're not. Only by doing this will you pinpoint all your weaknesses and develop a sound action plan to address them.

4. Schedule time in your calendar to perform a detailed Pipeline Review. Start by ensuring that each opportunity is in the correct buying-decision stage based solely on what your prospect is doing. Then, block times in your calendar each week for all the "big rocks" while leaving enough time in between for the small stuff. Do your best to stick with your plan and not get sidetracked by the many distractions that will undoubtedly arise.

CHAPTER 6

THE JOURNEY BEYOND

*"Success won't just come to you. It has
to be met at least half way."*

—FRANK TYGER

Congratulations! If you've read through the last five chapters
and got this far, you're on the path to greater selling success.
By applying the P3 Selling concepts consistently, you should
expect more self-confidence and a deeper sense of personal
satisfaction. And you'll be joining a select group of sellers that
have more control over achieving their goals versus just crossing
their fingers and hoping for a lucky break.

But now comes the hard part—making the P3 Selling strategies
work for you on an ongoing basis. Incorporating these strategies,
techniques, and processes into your day-to-day selling won't
happen automatically and will require some time and effort. So
our objective for this final chapter is to give you some tips on
how to do this. But first, let's recap what we've covered.

We started our journey by defining "selling" in contrast

to "Clerking." **Selling**, at its core, is about creating lightbulb moments—increasing a prospect's awareness of the need to change their thinking or situation through a combination of asking and suggesting. On the other hand, Clerking is about giving information and then closing for either the order or a commitment to the next buying step. Clerking assumes a prospect is already sold, so there is little need to influence them further. A closing question essentially asks, "Are you sold?" or at least, "Are you sold enough" to continue to the next step?

In B2B sales, Clerking tends not to work very well, particularly in decisions that involve complex products and buying processes. That's because being "sold" rarely happens after simply sharing some information, no matter how great it is. Unfortunately, this is the world in which most B2B sellers live.

There are three primary categories of activities within B2B selling: understanding, influencing, and messaging. The question then becomes, what exactly are you trying to understand, influence, and message? That's when I introduced the foundational concept of the **P3 Selling** method, which requires sellers to focus on three areas: a prospect's **Problems, People, and Processes** as they relate to purchasing the seller's products or services. These are the areas to understand, influence, and message. I then drilled down into each of these separately.

In our discussion on **Problems**, I pointed out that prospects don't really buy products or services. In reality, they buy solutions to problems or ways of capturing opportunities. Collectively, we called these "Problems." But the fact is that people and companies have lots of Problems that they aren't very motivated to address. So the job of selling begins with understanding a prospect's perspectives of their Problems and then influencing them on the Importance of addressing them. And you don't do this by telling but by asking. So what do you ask about? Early in a sales cycle, just three things: Facts, Problems, and Importance. But remember:

FACTS PROVIDE CONTEXT AND ENABLE YOU TO QUOTE. UNDERSTANDING PROBLEMS ENABLES YOU TO SELL, WHILE UNDERSTANDING A PROBLEM'S IMPORTANCE ENABLES YOU TO MOTIVATE.

Having a deep understanding of a prospect's perceptions of these allows you to develop a compelling message centered around what they want to buy rather than what you have to sell. I then shared a few Sales Plays, such as the Ask↔Suggest:Recap, or ASR, model, to help uncover, clarify, and increase the awareness of a Problem and its Importance.

I then referenced research on the typical number of **People** involved in a company's buying decision. In recent years, it has increased to ten or more, but most sellers focus their selling efforts on just one or two of them. This leaves them at considerable risk because they may not understand, nor have an opportunity to influence, the majority of these individuals' perceptions. However, at times, there will be too many people to connect with, so it's important to prioritize them based on two factors: the likelihood that they will participate in the buying decision, and your estimation of their Decision Influence. I also described several strategies on how to gain access to these people.

I also pointed out that in today's organizations, the buying-decision **Process** is the decision-maker—it is what links People and Problems with Action. There are two separate decision Processes that sellers need to understand, influence, and message—one for individuals involved in the buying decision and another for the company as a whole. It's important to align one's selling activities to where each individual and the company is in its decision Process and avoid making solution proposals too soon. It's also essential for all proposals to follow the flow of the buying-decision Process. This helps reinforce and validate the natural journey that each buyer takes.

Today, many company's buying Processes are overly complex and confusing due to the sheer volume of information and options available. As a result, a seller's primary role should be to act as the buying-Process expert for their specific offerings. This involves providing guidance on typical Problems, why they are important, and whom they tend to impact. They also need to advise on information to consider, options to explore, and selection criteria to use in order to arrive at the best decision. Sellers also want to encourage their contacts to engage Process People early, let them know what to expect, help resolve roadblocks, and collaboratively develop a plan that keeps the Process moving.

Lastly, I shared the **P3 Selling Playbook**, which describes the four most critical sales processes sellers need to know and regularly use to achieve consistent success.

Prospecting regularly and consistently is a key component of making most sales goals, so it's essential to do it well. Good prospecting involves creating interest in Problems you can address AND qualifying a prospect regarding their interest and ability to solve them. Prospecting success factors include pre-prospecting research and warm-up, compelling and concise messaging, engaging delivery, and following a consistent cadence.

Call management guides a seller on how best to plan and conduct each sales call to maximize the chances of moving a buying decision forward. We rarely have enough valuable face-to-face time with our prospects, so making every call count is critical. By establishing call objectives, ideal outcomes, areas to explore, and proposals to present before each call, sellers will find it easier to document and follow a professional and effective call flow.

Opportunity management is a process designed to maximize your chances of winning your most important sales opportunities. It involves understanding where you are in the buying-decision Process, developing a set of activities that align with that position, and executing action plans that move the deal forward. Key elements of opportunity management are the P3 Selling Deal Review process and the supporting tables that help define a buyer's decision stage and the associated selling objectives and activities.

Pipeline management helps sellers prioritize their activities to ensure a steady flow of sales revenue. It also provides an estimated forecast of near- to mid-term expected sales performance. Successful pipeline management is highly dependent on designating the correct buying stage for each opportunity and regularly conducting Pipeline Reviews.

P3 SELLING SUCCESS

Once you're confident that you understand the P3 Selling concepts, strategies, processes, and techniques, follow these few suggestions on how to make them part of your daily routine.

BECOME AN EXPERT ON THE PROBLEMS YOU SOLVE

For today's seller, a focus on solving customer Problems must be at the center of their universe because this is the foundation upon which everything else depends. Without the context of trying to solve one or more Problems, any discussion around product, price, options, People, or decision Processes makes no sense—zip, zero, zilch. When I shared this with a friend of mine, she wrote the following statement on a sticky note and pasted it to her computer screen:

UNTIL YOU'VE IDENTIFIED ONE OR MORE PROBLEMS THAT YOUR PROSPECT WANTS TO ADDRESS, YOU CANNOT SELL!

Whatever you can do to keep this concept top of mind will be key to your success. Becoming an expert on solving Problems involves more than simply listing them. You'll need detailed knowledge of why these Problems are important, whom they often impact, and the options available to deal with them. It's also imperative to understand which Problems you solve better than your competitors. That's because you'll want to spend more time understanding, influencing, and messaging to these rather than the ones anyone can address. If there's any part of this that you're unsure of, ask your co-workers and current customers.

Your goal is to understand these Problems better than both your prospects and your competition and then lead every selling interaction from the perspective of creating awareness of the need to solve them.

SET ASIDE TIME TO PLAN

As I said earlier, planning doesn't come naturally to most of us, and it's never as fun as just jumping into a selling situation and "letting the fur fly." The problem is that the outcomes are rarely as successful as they would have been with just a little bit of advanced planning. Planning doesn't always have to be a big ordeal—sometimes, just ten to fifteen minutes is enough. However, if it's a situation that's really important and your job or upcoming car payment depends on it, spending the extra time will almost always pay big dividends. The four areas that benefit greatly from planning are prospecting, customer calls, Deal Reviews, and Pipeline Reviews. I describe the planning process for each of these in the P3 Selling Playbook. Developing a high-level plan is often all you need for less critical sales calls. And planning for smaller deals is primarily about ensuring your activities align with the prospect's decision stage. Must-win deals, critical sales calls, prospecting, and Pipeline Reviews will always require a more significant investment in planning time to ensure your success.

REFLECT ON YOUR PROGRESS

Early on, it's difficult to know for sure if you're really making progress. We work hard at making calls and putting together proposals, glance up at the scoreboard at the end of each month or quarter, then put our heads down again, hoping to make our numbers for the next reporting period. But the numbers are just a reflection of our ability to perform a wide range of different activities. As such, it's essential to periodically stop and ask yourself which ones you do well and which ones could you do better. The psychologist John Dewey noted that "We don't learn from experience—we learn from reflecting on experience." For sure, there are many different sales activities you could reflect on. To make things easier, I'd like to suggest you start by regularly assessing your performance in just two areas: Sales Call Effectiveness and Pipeline Health.

A rough way to measure **Sales Call Effectiveness** is by asking yourself how often you realize your high-level call plans. Specifically, how frequently do you achieve the call objectives and outcomes you set to move the buying decision forward. If you believe it to be less than 75 percent of the time, look for ways to improve. Typically, this involves either asking better questions to understand and influence a prospect's Problems, People, and Processes or suggesting more compelling proposals that link to these areas. In most cases, developing better call plans or practicing specific selling techniques is the answer.

Pipeline Health offers a broader assessment of how you're performing. While a Pipeline Review tells you whether you have enough opportunities to make your numbers, it doesn't tell you how they should be distributed across the four decision stages. To assess your Pipeline Health, look for stages where you either have very few opportunities or where many of your deals seem to cluster. Sellers often have gaps in their early pipeline stages that commonly point to insufficient or poorly executed prospecting. This situation can be resolved by either improving your prospecting message and process or simply dedicating more time to it. Later-stage gaps or clusters occur when opportunities stall, often indicating misaligned selling activities. Getting ahead of your prospect in their decision process can cause them to stop, pull back, or even abandon the process entirely. If you're experiencing this, revisit the opportunity management tables in the Playbook to confirm you're doing the right things at the right times. If you're unsure of the best practices associated with any particular activity, refer back to the chapter that addresses it for a refresher.

Your journey to sales excellence will not happen overnight. But by simply changing your perspective from selling products to solving Problems, you should expect to see an almost immediate difference in how prospects perceive and value you. And by taking the time to plan and reflect on your progress, the P3 Selling concepts and techniques will eventually become second nature, enabling you to join the ranks of the elite professional sellers.

As your sales career progresses, there will be more advanced strategies and skills that you'll want to learn, such as key account management, contract negotiations, sales management, and even channel partner management. But proficiency in each of these will depend heavily on how well you have mastered the foundational P3 Selling concepts detailed in this book. So in closing, I'd like to leave you with one final thought:

YOU CAN TELL PEOPLE HOW GOOD YOU ARE, OR
YOU CAN SHOW THEM HOW GOOD YOU ARE.

My hope is that by applying the strategies, processes, and techniques outlined in this book, you'll deliver on the latter. Make it so!

P3 SELLING RESOURCES

Ready to start making P3 Selling work for you? To help get off to a fast start, go to www.P3Selling.com, where you can sign up to receive program updates and download free P3 Selling tools.

Here's a summary of the valuable resources you'll find:

- P3 Selling Key Concept Mini-Posters

- Chapter 2
  - Sample Problems and Opportunities to Ask or Suggest

- Chapter 5
  - P3 Selling Call Planning Template
    - High-Level Call Plan
    - Detailed Call Plan
  - Defining the Buying-Decision Stage Table
  - Establishing Selling Objectives and Key Activities Table
  - P3 Selling Deal Review Process
  - P3 Selling Pipeline Review Process

Have a question, comment, or suggestion? Send us a note at www.P3Selling.com—we'd love to hear from you.

NOTES

1   Hisaka, Alex. "LinkedIn's Definitive Guide to Selling to Multiple
    Decision-Makers." LinkedIn. Accessed February 14, 2022. https://
    business.linkedin.com/content/dam/me/business/en-us/sales-solutions/
    resources/pdfs/linkedins-definitive-guide-to-selling-to-multiple-
    decision-makers.pdf.

2   Sullivan-Hasson, Elizabeth. "The 2021 B2B Buying Disconnect." Trust
    Radius. November 10, 2020. https://www.trustradius.com/vendor-blog/
    b2b-buying-disconnect-2021.

3   Ibid.

4   "New B2B Buying Journey & Its Implication for Sales." Gartner.
    Accessed March 1, 2022. https://www.gartner.com/en/sales/insights/
    b2b-buying-journey.